D1178941

# SUNSET HOUSE

## More Perfume from Provence

# Sunset House

## More Perfume from Provence

*by*

THE HONOURABLE

## LADY FORTESCUE

*With Frontispiece and Jacket by*
E H. SHEPARD

William Blackwood & Sons Ltd.
Edinburgh and London
1937

# CONTENTS

vii

# CHAPTER I.

## LITTLE SUNSET HOUSE.

IN restless mood I was wandering one summer evening along the side of one of our loveliest mountains, through thickets of wild lavender, magenta gladioli, myrtle, thyme, and trailing sweet peas, when suddenly I came upon a little stone house perched upon a terrace overlooking a wide expanse of mountain ranges, valleys, and olive groves.

To its right, up aloft, was throned an ancient village, a tumble of crooked roofs and quaint gables ; crowning a lower peak was another tiny one with a slim, oblong, thirteenth-century clock-tower, a little four-square Mairie, and a few small cottages studding the slope of the hill. Vaguely beyond lay a distant town, nestling upon the bosom of a great mountain backed by the beautiful line of the Esterels and the misty sea.

My little cottage, squatting upon a ledge of rock, seemed to be gazing sleepily at this wonderful view, lulled by the music of water trickling into the great square basin at its side and the *cigales* in the woods around it. " Little sunset house of hearts standing all alone . . ." I quoted softly to myself as I looked upon it and loved it.

It was built of rough stones of every size and hue, and the irregularity of its shape enchanted me. Sloping roofs of old Provençal tiles, weathered to lovely tones of grey, ochre, and rose, covered the different levels of the rooms ; a crazy stone stairway led to a door on the eastern side, and another, on a lower southern terrace, climbed up to a small stone platform trellised over with vines. Clusters of purple grapes hung temptingly above the heads of two Italian babies playing lazily with a puppy in the sunshine. To the north, sloping roofs of lovely line covered a ruinous cart-shed fronting a rough courtyard. It was quite adorable this cottage, and, coming upon it unexpectedly, I experienced a queer sensation of possession, although it was obviously inhabited and I knew nothing of its past or present history. But I must know it and I must possess it.

These convictions came to me quite suddenly with the certainty that I must leave the loved Domaine that " Monsieur " and I had made together if I were ever to make anything of what remained to me of life. In fresh surroundings, free of those incessant haunting memories that hurt, I could perhaps work and continue to live. Between the dear walls of the Domaine I lived always in the past with a beloved ghost. He was ever so gallant that I knew he would deplore anything that sapped my courage, and, for two years since he left me, life at the Domaine had nearly killed my fighting spirit. I could not bear the loneliness within it, and, when I fled away from that empty chair, that collection of soldier portraits, his "Gallant Company" that he so loved; those shelves of military books; that great writing-desk, now neat and orderly, once piled with maps and quill-pens, compasses, chalks, papers and books of reference, I was always haunted by a feeling that I ought to be in his Domaine, guarding his home and his precious possessions. Then I would come back again— only to be defeated once more. Now, this little cottage seemed to say to me, "I will give you sanctuary—take me and love me and I will give you peace. Look how cosy I am! Inside me you will find great open fire-places and the ancient things you love. My walls are a metre thick, strong enough to protect you from all harm. You know his only wish was ever for your happiness. Make your decision now. Take me and you will never regret it."

I made it, then and there.

3

But I found that it is far easier to decide to buy an old Provençal cottage than to conclude the purchase. I asked the friends with whom I was staying if they knew to whom this adorable little place belonged, and discovered that the owner was their washerwoman.

" She wants to sell it, but has inflated ideas. She'll ask an enormous price," they informed me.

My hostess, whom I will call Mademoiselle, volunteered to approach Madame Pagini indirectly over the soap-suds while she was washing next day, and I, watching from a window, saw a massive woman in very rusty black with an incredible straw hat crowned with torn tulle, emerge from the laundry wiping strong brown arms upon her black apron in answer to the call of Mademoiselle.

From my vantage place I could see all but hear nothing ; however, in Provence one gathers quite a lot from animated gestures and the expression of the peasant as he—or she—listens, and I learned from the countenance of Madame Pagini that the questions of Mademoiselle were rousing hopes long dormant. Yes, she was anxious to sell her cottage ; but she asked a ridiculous price. Her husband had connected water to it and even electricity (one lamp in the kitchen), so that the purchaser would be saved much trouble and expense ; there were two thousand square metres of land, well cultivated, with walls all in good condition.

When Mademoiselle expostulated that the price was very high in these days, Madame Pagini explained that she and her husband were farming some land for a peasant proprietor who might put them to the door at any moment, and in this event if they had sold their cottage, they must have money enough to build another for their old age. At present their ancient home was inhabited by a nephew and his family who tended the land in return for free lodging. If the cottage were sold, of course, these tenants could be parked elsewhere.

All this was recounted to me by Mademoiselle, who said she was sure the price would descend if we remained firm and did not appear too keen ; for, although Madame Pagini had contrived to control her voice (a thing rare among peasants), she could not control the excited glitter of her eyes nor her eager fingers which pleated and re-pleated her dirty apron as she talked. The transaction might take weeks or even months to complete, but the cottage was as good as mine already if I wanted it.

If I wanted it . . . ! I had not dreamed that I could ever want anything so much again.

That night I stole out into the moonlight,

5

climbed the mountain path leading through my
hostess's property, in order to approach 'my'
cottage from the other side. I came to a low
boundary wall shaded by oak trees and wild
cherry, and through a vista of olive trees casting
queer twisted shadows upon a series of grass-
grown terraces, I saw "the little house of hearts
standing all alone," white, in the moonlight.

I clambered over the wall into this strip of olive
grove, which slid downhill from a great sloping
bank of huge grey boulders. Of course, this piece
of land must also belong to the Pagini property
since it adjoined the jessamine terraces below the
house and was divided only by a precipitous
path. What a marvellous natural rock-garden
one could make of that great sloping bank, planting purple Provençal iris on its crest where the
sun could shine through their petals; cascades
of aubretia of every hue, and white-flowered,
silver-leaved cerastium to ripple over those grey
rocks; wild violets, cyclamen, primroses, and
narcissi in the leaf-mould under the trees, and
clumps of Madonna lilies (which grow wild along
the streams of Provence) against the walls of grey
boulders under the cherry trees. I longed to begin
at once. The tangle of brambles, sarsaparilla,
and scrub must be cleared away; the clumps of
cystus and wild lavender left, of course. On one

of the lower terraces under the olive trees I would cultivate rows of Russian violets which, from above, would be seen as a purple carpet and not as stripes of colour ; and I would certainly plant a fig tree or two here and there at odd corners. I crept stealthily on, fearing to rouse the mongrel watch-dog chained to one of the iron supports of the vine pergola which covered the little stone platform. The last thing I desired was to see a half-naked Italian peasant emerge from the door and fire his gun into the air ; a pleasant habit of the species when scared.

I managed to approach quite near to the little house and stood under a gnarled fig tree looking across the valley to the nine lights of the topmost village and the three of our own, like stars against the soft darkness of mist - shrouded mountains. The scent from those little jessamine terraces was intoxicating. At rhythmic intervals the searchlight from the lighthouse at Antibes cut a radiant semicircle across the shadowed landscape, pointing a distant silver finger towards the little dreaming house as though repeatedly urging me to make it mine.

Well, I would start negotiations with Madame Pagini on the morrow. If I wanted flowers next spring I must make my preparations at once.

I walked down the mountain dreaming of all

that I would do when once this divine little property became mine, and burst into the Château below to rave to my two friends for an hour over that little stone cottage. They advised me to let our American man of law negotiate with the Paginis, who might easily try to *rouler* a lone woman. Also they mistrusted my enthusiastic mood. If I talked to the Paginis as I was talking now, the price would soar high. Accordingly an appointment was made for our lawyer and the two peasants who arrived clad in their best clothes, bringing a nephew with them as interpreter, for Monsieur Pagini only talked Provençal.

We shut the party into the secret walled garden of Mademoiselle, there to wrangle in private. I tried to spy and to eavesdrop from a window overlooking the garden, but my view was blocked by a gigantic fig tree, and the only voice that I could hear well was that of our man of law. I heard him tell Monsieur Pagini that his teeth were too long, and I heard the nephew retort that his uncle had but *one*. The rest of the conversation was drowned in laughter.

Evidently Monsieur Pagini was sticking out for an unreasonable price, but I was relieved to find that our American lawyer had lived long enough in the south of France to understand that

the best way of conducting business with the
Provençaux is to joke with them.

The most disquieting piece of information
elicited from this interview was that the inter-
vening strip of olive grove which joined the
Château property belonged to yet another peasant,
by the name of Froissart, who had once shared
the double cottage with Pagini. The dividing
wall of the house had at one time fallen down,
and, according to the Act signed by both men,
they were equally responsible for the repair of
this barrier. Pagini, being anxious to rid himself
of Froissart who had proved to be a cantankerous
neighbour, persuaded a builder friend to give him
an extortionate estimate of the price of repairing
the wall. Froissart, after seeing it, offered his
half of the cottage to Pagini for the sum of fifty
francs. Needless to say, the offer was swiftly
accepted ; but Pagini, not wanting more land
for himself, did not buy the strip of olive grove
adjoining his jessamine terraces. This was therefore retained by Froissart with the right of
passage down the little precipitous path between
the Pagini property and this bit of land, so that
he could always have access to tend his olive trees
and gather their crop.

Our lawyer, realising the importance to me of
this otherwise worthless piece of uncultivated

land, for old Froissart was lazy and had never pruned or cultivated the few meagre olive trees thereon, made its acquisition a condition of purchase. Without it, he explained to Pagini, Madame would not buy. She wanted a private passageway to the Château, and she did not want Froissart and his family continually pervading the property and trailing down the little path which, at one point, passed quite close to the house itself.

Pagini promised to negotiate for this bit of land, saying nothing of my desire to purchase his house, but pretending that he had reconsidered his decision and now wanted the olive grove for himself. It had originally been offered to him for three hundred francs.

The report of the negotiations was to be given to us within a few days ; but in the meantime Madame Pagini had confided to all her friends and relations in the neighbourhood that I had made an offer for their little property, and, needless to say, the rumour reached Froissart the same evening.

He was frantic. He had sold his share of this house for only fifty francs. Now it appeared that the old ruin was of value and that a mad Englishwoman wanted to buy it. He had lost the chance of pocketing perhaps thousands of francs which would now only enrich those cursed Paginis.

So that when Pagini visited him with his innocent request to buy the olive grove, cunning old Froissart burst into a roar of laughter and then told him to go to the devil. Tapping his red nose he informed Pagini that he was lying and that it was the English widow who wanted to buy his land. Well, she could have it for thirty thousand francs ; that was his price and also his last word. If she wanted to deal with him she could come in person.

Pagini, frustrated and furious, funked telling me this lest it should discourage me from buying his house, and we at the Château waited in suspense for weeks, not daring to make further inquiries lest we should appear too keen and the exorbitant prices remain fixed.

Then there came a day when poor Madame Pagini could bear the situation no longer. She appeared early one morning and demanded audience of Madame. I received her in the great salon, and seated upon a wide rush-bottomed chair, her sturdy legs thrust out wide before her encased in darned black stockings, her poor ace-of-clubs feet bursting through her black *pantoufles,* and her incredible hat perched on the back of her head, she poured forth the whole story of Froissart's *mechantisité.* He hated her and her husband, and this was his act of vengeance.

She implored me to buy their property and ignore Froissart, who, she was sure, would come to me afterwards, hat in hand, and beg me to buy his strip of land for nothing at all when he saw that his *coup* had failed.

But "once bitten twice shy." I remembered that when we had bought the Domaine we had been anxious to acquire two or three terraces below our garden belonging to another peasant. Directly he realised this his price soared to the Heavens so that we were advised to complete the purchase of the Domaine and treat with this peasant in years to come when he had learned reason and lost hope. But every Sunday afternoon, when "Monsieur" and I were peacefully working in our garden, the cunning old fox came with his complete, squealing family, camped upon his terraces below us, and lit evil-smelling bonfires which poisoned the atmosphere and invariably smoked us out.

The nuisance became unbearable and we were soon forced to buy his land if we wished to enjoy our Domaine in peace. I decided that nothing should persuade me to risk another such experience, and the chronicles of Froissart as recounted by the perspiring Madame Pagini made me less and less anxious to have him for a neighbour.

From this conversation with Madame Pagini

I realised that I must approach Froissart myself, a thing I had wished to avoid, for he was reported to be a little mad—or bad (the difference of only one letter)—and from glimpses I had seen of him trespassing amid the Château vineyards, I thought that I had seldom seen anyone less prepossessing. He lived in a ruined *cabanon* just below them, but shared meals with an ancient crone, whom he adored, in a little house a few terraces higher up.

Whether it was deliberate policy on his part or mere accident, I know not, but from the moment I made my decision to visit him, Froissart became invisible. I scrambled down to his house one morning and called his name—complete silence. I peered through the broken windows, but saw only bare planks and cobwebs. I climbed up to the house of his old lady friend, but she told me, with a glint of triumph in her eye (for my visit, of course, told her that I was anxious to buy his property), that Monsieur Froissart had gone to help a friend with his *vendange*.

When would he return? Who could tell? Much depended upon the quantity of grapes to be picked, and, when the picking was finished, he might be required to crush the grapes—and after that they would doubtless all drink to the success of the vintage and then—sleep. *Le bon*

*Dieu* alone knew when Monsieur Froissart would return.

Whether he did return and lay hid, just to tantalise me, I shall never know, but Mademoiselle's cosy old *bonne*, Asunta, was convinced that he was in hiding in his *cabanon*, and she haunted the piece of ground abutting upon the Château property, on the pretext of picking hazel nuts, so that she might spy out the land for me in the intervals of preparing delicious Italian dishes for our delectation.

One evening she suddenly became convinced that Froissart was within his house. She came up to the salon after dinner, looking quite beautiful in her dress of gentian blue cotton, her blue *pantoufles* to match, and her spotless white apron, and stood in the doorway, the light shining upon her mass of smooth, white hair, her strong brown arms folded across her ample tumpkin, and her yellow-brown eyes aglow.

Asunta's face is like a sun-kissed apricot, and that night it was flushed with excitement. She let loose a torrent of Italian-French upon us in a loud, mysterious whisper as though Froissart himself were just outside the front door. She implored Madame and Mademoiselle to make an expedition with her through the olive groves to his cottage so that we might all three beard him together. She dived into the hall and returned swinging a lighted lantern to encourage us to make this adventure.

We were washed out of the salon and into the courtyard by her flood of eloquence, and found ourselves groping our way through the trees, descending a narrow, stony path, scrambling down terraces, following Asunta, who went ahead so rapidly with the lantern that its light was entirely useless to us.

After my second tumble I became almost hysterical and felt sure that if I ever *did* arrive at Froissart's house I should be totally unable, after this undignified descent, to parley with him. Mademoiselle was better off: she was familiar with the holes in her path, the zigzags of its formation, and the gaps in her walls. She went ahead of me with a sure, light tread, hissing encouragement over her shoulder and gurgling with laughter at my muffled imprecations as I stumbled over a boulder or slipped on the dew-wet grass.

I managed at last to catch up with her, and we reached the house to find old Asunta bent double in her efforts to spy upon Froissart through the broken panes of his window. I asked her what we were to do if he were already in bed, and she said it would be excellent if he were, because he would not dare get out of it to dress himself in our presence and we could stay by him, keeping him a prisoner between the sheets—if he had any, *pauvre malheureux*—until he came to reason. But the door was bolted against such a surprise attack, and although she called his name loudly and even put her hand inside the broken windows to swing the lantern around his rooms, she failed to discover Froissart, and we all returned, defeated, to the Château.

It was several days later that I ran him to earth one evening in the old crone's cottage where they were supping onion soup before a wide, open fireplace. I liked his face even less upon close proximity ; the eyes were set too close together, which gave him a foxy look, and he had the most horrible hands I have ever seen, weird griping hands, more like the claws of some predatory bird.

However, he received me quite civilly, even jovially, and pronounced himself perfectly ready to treat with me for his olive grove if I would give him time to consider the matter (*oh*, these endless delays !) and make a formal appointment to receive him at the Château.

We made one for the following day, and Mademoiselle, knowing the customs of the peasants, bought a large bottle of vermouth to regale him during the interview.

He arrived punctually, washed but somewhat
unbuttoned, and once installed in a comfortable
chair began to blather about his great respect
for Mademoiselle (upon whose property he regularly
trespassed), saying that were it not that I was a
friend of hers he would never even consider giving
up his land. When we asked its price he stated
a far less fantastic sum, though much in excess
of the value of the land. We told him that we
had first heard that he was asking thirty thousand
francs, whereupon he burst into a roar of laughter
and informed us that he wanted to enrage Pagini,
who for the second time had deceived him,
and that he would only do business directly
with us.

Mademoiselle gently told the old man that the
value of the land was but three hundred francs,
the price he had originally asked Pagini, but
Froissart merely tapped his old nose and firmly
repeated his present price.

Mademoiselle told him this was absurd ; that
she knew that he knew it was absurd ; whereupon
he rose to his feet and with as much dignity as
his slipping trousers would permit, shuffled to
the door. With a quick movement she reached
it before him, closed it with a smile, led him back
to his chair, poured him out a glass of vermouth
—and then the discussion began all over again.

He told us frankly that he wished to profit over this transaction as well as Pagini ; that pernod was his favourite drink (unfortunate that we should have bought vermouth), and that he wished to make enough money to enable him to drink as much pernod as he liked till the end of his days.

We offered him one thousand francs, more than three times the value of his land, and pointed out that he would be able to line his cottage with bottles of pernod for that sum.

Again he rose to his feet to make for the door, stubbornly repeating his price, and this time noticing with dismay that the interval of visible shirt above trousers and below coat was lengthened by at least six inches, I signalled frantically to Mademoiselle, who, seeing the danger, rushed to a bookcase and turned her shaking back towards us while we let the old man depart with a cheerful word of farewell.

I rushed to a room whose open windows commanded a view of the drive, and was just in time to see the old villain throw his arms into the air and to hear him say to himself, " *Quelle blague !* " as he departed. I wondered whether he referred to our conversation or to his own as humbug or bunkum.

Again a deadlock. Poor Madame Pagini suffered

as much as I. She haunted the vicinity of the Château and cut her washing days in half, coming in the morning and leaving at mid-day so as to have an excuse to be permanently near her would-be buyer. Whenever by chance we met, our eyes signalled the same question—my eyebrow involuntarily shot up and her monstrous hat slipped farther back on her head as she tilted it acutely in the hope of news. Monsieur Pagini visited me and lowered his price, thinking that this might influence me to buy the cottage without Froissart's land, but I remained firm.

At last, rendered desperate by these delays, for if I were to inhabit the cottage the following year I must start its repairing and arranging at once before the wet weather set in, I called in a very charming French neighbour, Monsieur Packard, who, having lived in Provence all his life, could speak Provençal fluently and also, having stayed in London for a year, could understand English. I felt that he, if anyone, might be able to anchor old Froissart to some decision and act as interpreter for the bargaining parties.

He set to work at once, chasing old Froissart in a gallant little car from one peasant property to another, for the cunning old man who had not done a stroke of work for years had realised the importance of being elusive, and now engaged himself to help his neighbours with their wine-making so that he was never at home when we wanted to see him.

However, my persistent Frenchman at length ran him to earth and actually pinned him down to a fairly reasonable price for his strip of olive grove, even extracting from him a promise that he would come to the Château next day, receive a sum of money in advance of purchase from me, and sign a receipt for it in the presence of witnesses.

I was jubilant. At last it seemed that the cottage, plus the little ' Naboth's vineyard,' were to be mine, and Mademoiselle and I awaited the arrival of Froissart, who was to appear in company with our energetic Frenchman the next evening at six o'clock.

Punctually at six o'clock by Greenwich time we heard the clocks of the distant town strike the hour, but we knew that we must wait first for the bell of a neighbouring village to toll it five minutes later, and finally for that of our tiny hamlet to chime six times, ten minutes later than the bells of the town, for Froissart naturally would obey the bell of his native village.

As it ceased tolling, there was a ring at the front-door bell, and we admitted our Frenchman —who was alone.

He was very hot and angry, and burst into

voluble French, declaring that he would no longer negotiate with Froissart, who had gone back on his word and once again pushed up his price.

"I told him that I was ashamed that he was a Frenchman," he said furiously, "that Frenchmen were men of their word—in short, I told him that he was not a man at all and that I never wished to see him again. And then I left the cottage and banged the door upon him. I am sorry, Madame, that I have failed you."

I felt like a punctured tyre. We all stared at each other blankly, but while I was trying to thank our kind mediator for his efforts on my behalf, there was a sudden rattling of the round corks slung and knotted upon ropes to form a fly-curtain over the front door.

Our Frenchman stiffened and pointed like a retriever, as the head of Froissart poked through the corks. The old man peered around the dim hall and then shuffled across it to the open doorway of the salon, and seeing his French antagonist seated there he shouted at the top of his voice, "*Je suis un homme !*"

He did not look like a man at that moment, hatless, unshorn, his hands gripping the air, his eyes bloodshot, and those lamentable trousers slipping—slipping——

"They're coming OFF," I hissed hysterically to

Mademoiselle, forgetting that our Frenchman understood English.

His face worked, and a discreet hand shot up to cover his twitching mouth. Then he whispered triumphantly to me, "It's all right now. I wounded him in a tender place. He could not bear my taunt that he was not a man. Now we can deal with him."

And we did.

I paid him money in advance and signed a promise to pay the balance when the Act was signed. He laboriously signed a receipt prepared for him by the Frenchman, losing yet another button from the region whence buttons most readily spring in the effort.

And then we relaxed in our respective armchairs, all smiling geniality, and clinking the inevitable glasses of vermouth one with another, drank to the peace and prosperity of the little property.

I did not sleep much that night, for I was so longing to impart my news to Madame Pagini, who was still wilting with suspense. To-morrow I should have the joy of announcing to her over the soap-suds that at last our agony was over and that there was nothing now to prevent my purchase of her cottage.

Next morning I watched her approach to the Château. Her sallow face was of an even unhealthier hue than usual under that deplorable hat—I noticed that the rusty tulle crown had exploded completely, perhaps with the ferment of anxiety inside the poor head, and a few wisps of greying hair sprouted through the aperture like a plume.  One bare toe had also sprouted through stocking and felt slipper, doubtless forced through by the many extra journeys she had made to the Château in the hope of news.  As she climbed the last ascent she stopped at intervals to wipe the sweat from a furrowed brow and to swivel beady black eyes around the property in search of me.

I ran out to her gaily, and directly she caught sight of my smiling face her own lit up.  She threw her arms wide into the air, then slapped them down upon her thighs, ejaculating—

" *Eh ben!* "

I nodded violently.

" *C'est fait ?* " she inquired hoarsely.  I nodded again more violently, and she plumped down upon a boulder in her favourite attitude, legs spread wide, elbows crooked, and hands on knees.  Her hat slipped off backwards and rolled unregarded down the mountain.

" *Pas possible ?* "

And then her mouth widened and widened, opened, to display the sad fact (which was her pride) that she had never visited a dentist in her life, and let forth a rumbling roar of triumphant laughter.

She laughed and laughed and laughed. She rocked forwards and backwards and from side to side, tears poured down her cheeks as she fanned herself with her dirty blue apron, waggling her head, speechless with emotion. Then I held out my hand, whereupon with a supreme effort she levered herself to her feet and clasped it in both hers, pumping it up and down as she repeated, "*Eh ben!* Eh ben!" in the familiar *patois* of Provence.

I recounted to her the final interview with old Froissart, and told her that the matter really was settled with him since he had signed a paper agreeing to a certain sum, had accepted some of the purchase money for his olive grove in advance, and had given me a receipt.

"Now when can you and your husband come down with me to Cannes to sign the Act for the purchase of the cottage?" I asked. "I will drive you both down in my car if you will fix a day."

Madame Pagini promised to go back at once and interview her husband—yes, he was sure to be at home and she would send me a message by Jules—her beautiful but extremely lazy son—during the morning. Then, after more hand-shaking, she departed, leaving Mademoiselle's household linen unwashed and forgotten in the laundry.

I had quite expected to hear that it would be impossible for Monsieur Pagini to visit the lawyer in Cannes until the following Monday, when he would have had his weekly shave, but apparently he and his wife decided that for this great occasion the expense of an extra shave (nearly every Provençal goes to the *coiffeur* for this weekly rite) was justified—or perhaps they feared that if they delayed four days I might change my mind ? Anyway, an appointment was made for the very next day for Monsieur and Madame Pagini to come to the Château and there embark in my car.

When they arrived they were beautiful to behold. Madame had covered up the deficiencies of her clothing with a cloak of rabbit-skins (doubtless poached by her husband) lent, as she confided to me later, by a married daughter who had also provided a hat of the latest mode which would have been very *chic* had it been worn at the correct angle over the eye and not on the extreme back of the head, and had it not been several sizes too small. To secure it at that perilous angle, a kitchen skewer had been pierced through it and the knob of hair at the back. Leather shoes completed the outfit.

25

Monsieur Pagini wore a dashing sombrero and a scarlet muffler worn around the throat to hide an extremely dirty flannel shirt and the lack of a collar. An orange marigold was stuck into the button-hole of his coat—the last *souci* that he ever hoped to bear.

I tucked them, side by side, into the back seat, where Madame Pagini sat rigid, majestically upright, hands folded in her lap, whilst her husband lolled luxuriously and asked my permission to smoke one of those small evil-looking (and smelling) cheroots beloved by all Italians. This he waved in nonchalant greeting to friends and relatives as we passed through our village, chuckling happily to himself as he received their rather sour acknowledgments of his salute, for there were many would-be vendors of property in the village since the buying of ancient cottages became the mad mode.

Once outside the village, I saw in the mirror before me that Monsieur Pagini's attitude became also still and tense, and, to my relief, he even forgot to puff at his cheroot, which gradually went out. His eyes were fixed upon the fleeting scene, and after a time the end of his hawk-nose was actually pressed against the window-pane. From time to time he gave an astonished grunt.

His wife's majestic pose never relaxed, but

two spots of colour burned in her sallow cheeks and her eyes rolled wildly from side to side taking in everything. Neither spoke.

At length I made some remark about the country we were passing through, whereupon Madame Pagini, without moving her head and scarcely moving her lips, told me in a noisy whisper that it was the first time her husband had ever been outside his village since he left Italy as a boy and that he was naturally a little overcome. The pathos of it. . . .

When we reached the outskirts of Cannes I noticed that Monsieur Pagini fumbled in his pocket, produced matches, and, with fingers that shook ever so slightly, lit again his poisonous cheroot, doubtless to give him confidence as he approached a big town. Understanding this, I contrived with an effort to conquer the feeling of nausea that even a good cigar arouses within me, and concentrated my mind wholly upon driving through the ever-thickening traffic.

We went first to the office of my American man of law who had treated (unsuccessfully) with the Paginis in the first instance. He greeted them charmingly as old friends, for which I was very grateful, for I saw that they immediately gained a little courage ; and together we all drove to the house of the French lawyer who had drawn

27

up the Act in readiness. Even I was scared by the magnificence of these palatial quarters, shared by many lawyers. A great square hall, floored with white marble and closed in on all sides by heavy glass doors framed in solid polished mahogany, was lined with enormous leather couches, upon the edges of which perched timorous waiting clients.

The eyes of the Paginis rolled reverently around as they tiptoed gingerly over that floor, Madame Pagini pausing after each step to dust with a perfectly filthy pocket handkerchief the places where their feet had left marks. Then we all perched likewise upon those imposing leather couches and waited our turn.

I saw that Monsieur Pagini was in difficulty about something, and suddenly realised that it was his extinct cheroot. He longed to light it, but dared not, yet equally he dared not throw it upon that marble floor. His desperate eye roved about in search of the convenient spitoon provided by all French *estaminets* and *cafés*, and, finding none, I saw him nudge his wife, who had resumed her former majestic pose. Without turning her head she squinted sideways in his direction, and seeing his dilemma, produced once more that dreadful handkerchief. Surreptitiously Monsieur Pagini handed her the sodden end of the cheroot, which she swiftly rolled up in a corner of that useful piece of linen, tying a substantial knot to keep it in safely. The handkerchief was then pushed into her pocket.

After a time a beautifully tinted young lady came through one of the glass doors and motioned us to follow her into the office of *Monsieur le Notaire*.

He greeted us casually, making us feel that we were only a tiresome little bit of routine business which must be disposed of as quickly as possible.

I suppose we were, but I hated him for snubbing poor old Madame Pagini, who began to tell him the story of her life, that her family had been born in the cottage which Madame had now bought, but that times being hard, they had quitted it to become the farmers of a neighbour with the idea of returning to their old home if he ever ' put them to the door,' or of selling it and with the money building eventually a small modern house for their old age. . . .

She began, smiling and confidentially, but at that moment the desk telephone rang, and with an imperious gesture *Monsieur le Notaire* bade her be silent while he discussed some important affair involving several millions of francs with an invisible colleague.

The eyes of Monsieur Pagini goggled with awe

29

and respect, but his poor wife merely mopped her dripping face with that useful handkerchief. The room was centrally heated to suffocation point, and she was obviously suffering in her fur cloak. Our kind American adviser seeing her distress, added to it unknowingly, by urging her to remove this (to him) unnecessary wrap. He could not know, poor man, the poverty this rich garment concealed.

Fortunately, the telephone conversation came to an end at this moment and *Monsieur le Notaire* could once more deal with insignificant affairs. He proceeded to read the Act aloud to all parties concerned, as is customary, and then Monsieur Pagini was asked to sign it. . . .

There was an awful pause, during which no one moved anything but anxious and inquiring eyes.

Our American friend produced an elaborate fountain-pen which he handed to Monsieur Pagini, thinking perhaps that this would encourage him, but the poor man merely looked desperately first at his wife and then at me as though imploring aid.

Perhaps it was the heat of the room, perhaps a little giddiness caused by Monsieur Pagini's cheroot, that had dulled my brain, for I could not imagine the cause of his reluctance to sign that Act till Madame Pagini, under cover of the handkerchief, whispered hoarsely to me that neither she nor her husband could read or write.

In English I hastily explained the difficulty to our American supporter, who tided over an embarrassing moment with one of his kindly jokes, and *Monsieur le Notaire* then superciliously wrote the signatures of the vendors, who afterwards affixed their mark of approbation. Lastly, I handed over the purchase money and obtained my receipt.

And so the matter was concluded and we could all adjourn to the nearest *café*, there to drink each other's healths.

The tongues of Monsieur and Madame Pagini were now unloosed. So chatty did they become that even when he had finished leisurely sipping his vermouth, our American adviser found it difficult to excuse himself from our company. As he half rose from his seat for the second time he was again detained by the now genial Pagini, who reminded him that he had not yet drunk with them to the peace and prosperity of Madame in her new home, and this was very charmingly done. . . .

That wished-for peace was destined to be short-lived. The very next morning it was destroyed.

Hardly had I had time to inspect my lovely little ruin or to dream of effects of colour that

I might gain in my garden; scarcely had Mademoiselle scribbled her first plan of the arrangement of rooms in my cottage—for she was to be my architect—when, whilst wandering in my newly acquired olive grove, I was surprised to receive a letter from *Monsieur le Maire*, brought to me by a little apple-cheeked boy.

I opened it hastily, wondering what rural law I could already have transgressed so soon to receive an official letter from the Mayor.

Its contents completely shattered me. He wrote, most kindly, to inform me that according to his *cadastre* (the map of numbered properties with the names of their owners inscribed thereon) the strip of olive grove for which he understood that I was in treaty with Froissart HAD BEEN SOLD TO ANOTHER CITIZEN OF OUR VILLAGE THREE YEARS AGO. *Monsieur le Maire* thought that he must warn me at once lest I fell a victim to trickery.

I sat down heavily upon a (pointed) rock, and that awful letter fluttered to the ground. Mademoiselle, engrossed in the inspection of the interior of the cottage, heard my cry of mental (and physical) pain, and hurried out into the garden in time to hear me exclaim—

" The old fox ! "

" Who is a fox ? " she asked in bewilderment.

" Now you're not going to tell me . . ." she began.

32

"Read that letter," I replied briefly, picking it up and handing it to her.

She first extracted and lit a cigarette, a sure sign of mental perturbation with her, then slowly read the letter.

"Ring up Monsieur Packard AT ONCE!" she commanded me curtly. "He is the only man who can deal with the old devil," and I obediently telephoned to our kind French friend and informed him of the catastrophe.

The telephone twanged like a Jew's harp with the vibrations of his furious voice. Although nearly deafened, I yet managed to gather the consoling assurance that he would get into his car at once and hunt that old fox of a Froissart to his doom.

Two hours later he arrived at the Château, moist but mollified. He had confronted that old man over his onion soup, of which he was partaking in company with the ancient crone who, extra-ordinarily, found favour in his eyes. Directly Monsieur Packard had voiced his accusation, old Froissart had risen from his chair with as much dignity as his slipping nether garments permitted, and had commanded the old lady to go upstairs at once to fetch the money I had already paid him, saying that if Madame distrusted his honesty he preferred to have no dealings with her.

The money was actually produced, but thank heaven Monsieur Packard was too astute to take it before he had verified Froissart's oath that he had NOT sold that strip of olive grove to any previous person. Years of experience of the Provençaux had taught him to know when they were speaking the truth and when lying, and he was now ready to swear that old Froissart was innocent and that some mistake of names must have been made by the surveyors in drawing up the *cadastre*.

And so it proved. Froissart had sold another piece of land three years ago, but had retained the strip of olive grove adjoining the Pagini land and the right of passage around the cottage and down the bordering path, chiefly, I expect, to be able to annoy the Paginis by his scoffing presence when he so desired.

And so the Mayor's letter proved to be a mare's nest, and after all there was nothing to prevent old Froissart and me from signing the Act of Purchase before his local lawyer at once.

But I found that this could not be performed at once. Another delay; but this one was merely caused by the fact that old Froissart only shaved once a fortnight, and the time was not yet. He must have a shaven chin " in order to kiss the widow " after the Act was signed, he jocularly informed Monsieur Packard, who, unkindly, told me.

I very nearly cancelled the whole arrangement, so great was my consternation—nay, horror ; for old Froissart has no water on his property, so that he has every excuse never to wash, and old Froissart dribbles and resembles a hairy ape rather than a man. " Not a fascinating citizen," as " Monsieur " would have described him. However, Monsieur Packard reassured me. The old man would never have the courage to put his threat into execution. He would be so overjoyed to get his *mille* notes that all else would be forgotten.

Nevertheless, I implored Monsieur Packard to accompany us on this expedition that the proprieties might be observed.

And so, the day after old Froissart's beard was harvested, we all three set off in Monsieur Packard's little car, bound for the lawyer's office.

We drove through golden and russet vineyards, through pungent pine-woods, snorted up hills, and raced through smiling valleys until we reached the ancient little town where lived Froissart's lawyer. Here we turned down a narrow cobbled street, under a great stone archway, and drew up at his door, where we descended and were delayed for some time because old Froissart kept recognising relatives and acquaintances. It was to this little town that the old reprobate trudged when he wanted a drink of his favourite pernod, our village boasting of no *café* or *estaminet*. He wanted to make the most of this great day. He was shorn and attired in his best clothes. He had been driven here in an automobile with an important man of business and an English widow. In a few moments he also would be a capitalist, for he had sold some property to that lady over there.

All this, so Monsieur Packard told me, was being confided to the people of the town, who poked old Froissart jovially in the ribs as he tapped his nose triumphantly and winked his wicked old eye.

But all things have an end—even the conversations of the Provençaux—and at last the old man rejoined us, and we rang the lawyer's bell and were admitted. We found him seated in a tiny dark office before an enormous antediluvian typewriter, a thin bespectacled young man, obviously quite terrified of me.

He gained a little confidence when I shook him by the hand, and Monsieur Packard greeted him cordially, as an old friend, and he began, haltingly, to read out the Act of Purchase that he had prepared.

Old Froissart drew his chair close up to the desk and sat opposite the *notaire,* his eyes glued upon the document as though they could read it upside down. After each phrase he nodded his head energetically, took a pinch of snuff and sneezed violently, which made the poor lawyer more and more nervous. In any case he was in difficulties over my name, which seemed to me curious, as it is a French one. First, I was Fortesque, pronounced like picturesque, then Fortes*cur,* and I had to explain to him that *cur* in English meant a *chien sans race,* which feeble joke plunged him into an agony of embarrassment and a tide of blushes, poor little man. I was spelt in at least five different ways in that one short document, and wondered which form I must use for my signature, as I seemed quite unable to correct the frightened man. However, Monsieur Packard came to the rescue once more, and taking the document from the *notaire's* nervous fingers, he wrote FORTESCUE in block letters above the variations, and I initialled the corrections.

Then old Froissart was called upon to sign this important paper, which he did with much waste of ink, even contriving to smear some upon his nose. Finally, I inscribed my name. The *notaire* then asked me to state my profession,

37

and while I hesitated Monsieur Packard gallantly suggested that I should designate myself as a *femme de lettres*. I hardly felt justified in describing myself as a woman of letters, having produced but one small book, but he insisted, and the pretentious title was written down by the *notaire*.

Some weeks later, in that same office, a peer of England who had also bought a small peasant property was asked to state his profession. After a moment of doubt he described himself as *pair d'Angleterre*. The little lawyer wrote *père d'Angleterre*, and was never corrected, for, after all, to be a tolerant and efficient father to a family of six modern children is, in itself, a full-time occupation.

The Act of Purchase duly signed by all parties, I rose and asked *Monsieur le Notaire* his fee. Twelve francs. Only twelve francs for all that agony !

I paid him this modest fee, and then asked him if he would do me the honour of accompanying us to the nearest restaurant, there to celebrate the signing of the Act. This I did out of mere politeness, not dreaming that so important a personage as the only lawyer of the town would leave his office on so frivolous an excuse.

But to my surprise he leaped to his feet, delight depicted on every feature, bowed to me repeatedly as he expressed his ecstatic thanks, took down a worn felt hat from a peg, and ushered us from the room and into the street, locking up the front door behind us with a ponderous key.

By this time the daylight had faded and a few lamps had been lit in the steep streets. The ancient shadowed houses, silhouetted against the afterglow, seemed to lean across and whisper to each other, for all were out of the perpendicular.

We traversed a little Square, walking under giant plane trees, climbed a rugged stone stairway inside the great archway through which we had previously passed, and reached a long raftered room set with marble-topped tables and flanked by a bar well furnished with bottles filled with many-hued fluids, through which the lamplight gleamed.

At the end of the room an Italian was playing gay music upon an accordion, and old Froissart's face lit with delight as he heard the favourite Provençal music.

We chose a table near a window in the centre of the archway looking down into the cobbled street, and I asked the gentlemen what they would like to drink.

Pernod—they all preferred pernod—and three glasses of wicked-looking green liquid were brought to us upon a little tray, and a tumbler of sickly bottled lemonade for me.

My companions all drank to my health and happiness in the new property that I had acquired. Long might I live to enjoy it. I thanked them all for their kindness and watched them tilt that fiery liqueur—a kind of absinthe—down their well-trained throats. Then I offered them all another glass. Only old Froissart accepted. Before we left he had imbibed four glasses of his beloved pernod and had grown loquacious and pathetic.

He told me that it was his great delight to come here and see a little life. At home nothing ever happened, and one saw the same few faces day after day, month after month, year after year. There was no *café*, no music, nothing to change the ideas. You rich people, he said to me, but without bitterness, when you are bored with the country, you get into your cars and you drive down to Cannes or Nice and amuse yourselves in the coastal towns, but we—we have to remain where we are and we turn into vegetables.

It is always the unattainable that seems attractive, I thought, for, as a matter of fact, we who have cars seldom use them to visit the gay Riviera towns. We go there if we need provisions, and then with heavy hearts, resenting the necessity of leaving our mountain homes and our gardens. But we do know that we *can* escape if we want to.

After his fourth glass of pernod old Froissart became sleepy. Even the antics of the *patron*, dancing to the strains of the accordion with his baby girl, failed any longer to divert him. It was time to go home. In the car he sat huddled in a corner, lovingly fingering his *mille* notes.

" A pernod every night, every night, as long as I live," he mumbled exultantly to himself.

# CHAPTER II.

## MADAME BECOMES A PEASANT PROPRIETOR.

THE cottage with its five little jessamine terraces and the coveted strip of olive grove were now mine beyond dispute. The Act had been signed and my parcels of land duly registered correctly upon the *cadastre* at the Mairie. I was now a citizen of the village.

I longed to begin the reconstruction of the little house at once. Madame Pagini had promised me that the moment I took legal possession, her nephew and his family, who had been occupying the cottage rent-free in return for farming the land, would go at once to the new home that had been found for them, which they would enjoy under the same conditions as before. Until they departed we realised that any minute inspection of the cottage, or any concentrated planning for its rearrangement, was quite impossible ; for the curiosity of these Italians was so insatiable that they dogged our footsteps and followed in a noisy chattering train wherever we went. It was impossible to hear oneself or others speak, or to move without stamping upon a baby, a cat, a dog, or a moulting hen, for they all lived together, squabbling and scratching in that ruinous interior.

One look at the one and only bedroom where the whole family slept was enough for me. The ceiling had half fallen in, and a truss of hay from the loft above was sliding through the aperture. The remaining planks were supported only by one rotting pillar of wood—and the large bed was placed immediately under this dangerous construction. It looked as though the next mistral would bring down the last remnants of rafters and plaster upon the poor little family huddled beneath.

It was almost incredible that children could live under such conditions. Naturally they looked sickly. Wondering whether that last grimy baby had been born in that still grimier bed, I shuddered and left the room, followed by Mademoiselle.

" Discouraged ?  A little ? " she whispered.

" I was thinking of those unfortunate children," I replied sadly.

" Awful," she agreed.  " But about this place ? "

" Well, of course, the whole cottage must be gutted—and disinfected," I replied.

" But the shell that will remain is solid," she comforted me. "Those walls are a metre thick, and just look at those glorious fireplaces. Oh, we are going to have such fun arranging it all." Her artist's eye glowed with enthusiasm as she gazed at the blackened rafters in the big kitchen, the jar built into the wall near the great fireplace, its rounded projecting side stamped with the seal of the monastery from which it came.

" In old days the peasants kept holy water in that jar," explained a friend who was with us ; " and since then it has been used for the family washing," commented Mademoiselle. " But look at that wonderful fireplace ! You must leave those great grey rocks at the back of it—part of the foundations of the cottage, for you'll find that it is built upon the solid rock of the mountain— OH ! what is that ? " she yelped as her legs were suddenly seized from behind by a sturdy young Italian.

" Only the ex-baby," I reassured her. Then, as I discovered its father standing at my elbow, his loose mouth hanging open, his eyes goggling with curiosity, and his slatternly wife clasping her latest child standing by his side, I exclaimed irritably : " Oh, let's go away. One can discuss nothing with this family trailing around after us."

Mademoiselle turned upon the father and asked him when he intended to move into his new home, reminding him that it was agreed that the moment Madame had signed the Act she was to have immediate possession of the cottage, and that the builders would be coming the next day to start pulling down the rotten ceilings. He smiled vacantly and waved large hands about him, saying that there was much still to be done before they could leave.

Then why didn't he start doing it ? she asked him briskly. He pointed to a sack of potatoes and a bale of hay that he had already dragged into the courtyard, and his wife nodded vigorously. Evidently they thought that they had accomplished a great deal in two days.

The next morning I climbed the terraces from the Château, hoping that I might find my cottage empty. I walked through my little bit of olive grove (which was especially dear to me because of the battle we had had to acquire it) with eyes on stalks and ears strained to listen for the dreaded sound of raised Italian voices.

Sure enough the familiar babel greeted me as I rounded the corner. The moment I came into view the mongrel cur of the peasant family rushed forth to greet me. Never having received a caress in his life before he had adopted Mademoiselle

45

and me as his own, as had the ex-baby, who
followed, likewise, at our heels, embracing our
knees with skinny arms whenever we came to
a standstill. This ex-baby roused my compassion
from the first, a little puny girl with enormous
eyes set in a pinched pale face. She was terribly
dirty and she was consequently whiffy, but infinitely pathetic. The mother, seeing that I was
interested in the child, tried to explain and to
exploit her. She told me that her little girl had
had double pneumonia and that a rib had been
removed to draw forth water from the lungs. She
pulled up the child's ragged frock—to my horror
there were no underclothes—and proudly displayed a horrible scar. Later, this tragic white
seam was shown to Mademoiselle and to all who
visited my cottage. The child looked, and I
believe was, half-starved, and so I brought her
up a tin of biscuits. A wolfish gleam came into
her eyes and she rushed off with it to a corner of
the garden, like a dog with a bone, returning ten
minutes later to brandish the empty tin before me
and scream hopefully : " *Biscottes ! Biscottes !* "

That Italian mother—though she hardly de-
served the sacred name—roused a whirlwind of
feeling inside me : irritation, pity, hot indignation—all kinds of conflicting sensations, she was
so hopelessly inefficient and slatternly. Although

that large stone basin containing twenty thousand litres of water adjoined the cottage, she had never had the energy or inclination to clean either her children or her home. She had nothing else to do, and did nothing but wandered aimlessly around clasping her dirty baby in her arms. Whenever she opened her mouth it was to scream harshly to her children, who, like all normal offspring, were for ever doing what they should not, and who continued to do it receiving only screams of admonition which soon died lazily away. Though there was an abundance of vegetables in the little garden this mother never troubled to make her family a good soup. All I ever saw there in the way of food was a saucepan full of potatoes boiling over a fire of sticks. Perhaps she had lost courage during the fight for life, and as I thought this, a surge of pity washed over me ; but even were this so, I felt very strongly that a woman blest with children might at least make some effort to cleanse and nourish them.

The father appeared to be half imbecile (I should have been quite had I been obliged to live with that woman), but he was sane enough to be anxious to shred from the little property every thing growing thereon before his departure.

The grapes had already been harvested, but there was still much else that might be taken away, and he was seeing to it that nothing should be left—and taking as long about it as he could in order to enjoy this novel form of entertainment that we were providing for him and his family. He was like the Psalmists' description of the Almighty, " about my path " (fortunately NOT " about my bed," except in the form of a nightmare) " and spying out all my ways." I think he wanted me to take him on as gardener, for he had been out of work for months, but I was already supplied with one, and in any case could never have borne his indolence and vacant grin.

Would they NEVER go ?

As the days went by, and still they were in occupation of my cottage, I began firmly to believe that this family of Italian peasants intended to remain with me for the rest of my life. Was it because they had become so attached to the old cottage that they could not bear to be uprooted, or was it, as I still believe, merely a hungry curiosity that impelled them to stay ?

We told them again that the masons were coming to start work at once, and that when they began destroying the rotting ceilings and dilapidated partition walls, the children would be in continual danger from falling débris. They MUST be removed at once.

The next day appeared Dante, the little Italian

mason, who had undertaken to rebuild the cottage under the direction of Mademoiselle. Nothing less Dante-esque could have been found in all the world. He was stumpy and square, and though still in the early forties, a little given to fat. In fact he formed a series of circles and contours, the face being round and chubby, the eyes completely circular, the nose like a button mushroom, the mouth almost spherical, and the tumpkin—— He was rubicund and smiling.

He knew nothing of architecture or design, but Mademoiselle had proved in the past that his work was solid and conscientious. This would be his first big job, and he evidently realised the importance of the occasion, for, although it was only Wednesday, he had had a shave and put on his best clothes for the interview : black cloth trousers, a coat with padded shoulders and a nipped-in waist, worn over a woollen pullover of orange with white stripes. A check cap, worn at a jaunty angle, completed this *festa* attire. A pencil was stuck behind a very pink ear to look business-like, and the inevitable Caporal cigarette swung from a corner of the mouth to give confidence. He was sweating with excitement.

We had prowled round my little place by moonlight when the Italian family were in bed, but had postponed the complete tour of the house

until we could make it in his company, and, as
we hoped, when it was empty of peasants, beasts,
and birds.

But to-day they were all present, the complete
menagerie, following, following, faithfully following.

With a stern effort Mademoiselle attempted to
concentrate upon the problem of rearrangement.
She made various inquiries as to the solidarity of
outside walls, and Dante tapped and found them
good. Then he proceeded to examine those of
the interior, which were one and all condemned.
The ruinous ceilings need not be considered, for
if left for a few weeks longer they would fall down
without help.

We decided that the adjoining kitchens of the
double cottage would form a hall dining-room
and a little salon; the dividing wall would be
partly built up again, leaving a square opening
so that the two rooms appeared as one. Each had
a beautiful open fireplace and glorious black oak
beams.

The queerest little stairway mounted to the
loft, irregular stone steps, crazily crooked, with a
rough wooden balustrade, the whole built over
a quaint half-arch recess in the wall. We climbed
this adorable construction and gingerly stepped
into the loft, peering through the gaping floor
into that deplorable bedroom beneath (which

would one day be my only guest-room) whilst standing upon the solid oak beams which supported what remained of rotten planks and plaster.

The loft ran the length of both cottages, but it was only possible to stand upright in the centre, the roof of lovely old, rounded, Provençal tiles sloping sharply to either side.

This roof must be heightened, decided Mademoiselle, and then there would be space enough for a bedroom, bathroom, and writing-room for me. Crouched on a beam she began swiftly to draw a design, when suddenly the head of the Italian papa poked through the aperture above the stairway, followed by his vile body.

He had only come to fetch some more hay, he explained affably, widening his legs so that one of his progeny should crawl through them.

Mademoiselle pettishly threw down her pencil and note-book. " It is *impossible* to do anything until this awful family clears out ! " she exclaimed in desperation.

The little mason pushed back his cap in offended surprise at the intrusion, stuck out his stomach, and dug two indignant thumbs into the armholes of his coat.

Then he addressed the interruption in his own fluent tongue. When at length he had expressed

his own opinion in his own way : " Tell him that
you are starting the work of demolition to-morrow,
and that if he and his family remain I refuse to
be responsible for their safety," I urged. But
though this was done, energetically enough, I
had little hope that my warning would be heeded.

" All we can do to-day is to inspect every hole
and corner of the place," I decided, " and WHEN this
family departs we can decide details of reconstruction and draw plans. At least you can
start pulling down the ruined masonry," I said
to Dante, " and if these people are still here to-
morrow, upon their own heads be it." He nodded
vigorously and we crawled down into the big
kitchen.

" Now comes the most exciting part of all,"
whispered Mademoiselle, " and do remember that
whatever lovely thing we find in those caves
beneath, DON'T exclaim in your usual foolish
and exuberant fashion, or that man," casting a
glance of hatred at the peasant papa always close
behind us, " will surely take it away with him,
or say that it belongs to him and try to make
you buy it. I know these people better than you
do." I gave a chastened promise to repress my
exuberance.

Beneath the second kitchen (soon to be the
salon) was hung an old sack which was obviously

placed there to hide something beneath. Cautiously I lifted it and saw, in a huge recess built in the thickness of the wall, a mother rabbit and her young. I quietly lowered the sack and passed on to a tunnelled passage from which emanated a decidedly piggy aroma. I followed the smell into the dim interior of a cave, stumbling over something extremely hard as I entered.

Lighting a match I discovered that this obstruction was the loveliest rugged stone trough, circular in form and about twelve inches thick. I only just repressed one of my prohibited squeals of delighted discovery and instead called to Mademoiselle in as casual a voice as I could muster.

Upon seeing my find she merely dug me sharply in the ribs, but the flicker of the match had shown me a glint in her eyes. The mason had followed her with a lighted candle which revealed another stone trough, oblong in shape and even heavier than the circular one. Two young pigs were sloshing up their morning meal mixed within it. I gazed entranced—at the receptacle—not the pigs.

" Look up. Can't you LOOK UP ? " urged the voice of Mademoiselle, and I looked up.

This cave was formed of loose boulders of every hue of grey, ochre, and rose, and at the back of it was a glorious rounded arch above a recess from which projected the rocks of the mountain, great grey rocks, rugged and lichened.

"What a possession," muttered Mademoiselle, and the Italian mason suggested that I should transform it into an Arab room like that under the Château of Mademoiselle.

In my heart I then and there decided to make it into a tiny primitive chapel and to dedicate it to the memory of the most wonderful parents child ever had, and the beloved "Monsieur." But at that moment I held my peace.

"That rabbitry could be made part of this," said Mademoiselle with an ecstatic enveloping sweep of the arms; "one need only poke out a few of those great stones to make a window."

A cloister for my chapel, I thought secretly. The pig perfume overcame me at that moment and forced me out into the open air, where a heady whiff of jessamine from my five little terraces revived me.

"There will be more caves under the next cottage," prophesied Mademoiselle, who had followed me out of the first.

"I suppose we must wait for Dante to emerge from that Inferno," I replied. "Evidently he is more accustomed to these perfumes of Provence than we." At that moment he emerged, lips

54

pursed with importance, to say that of course
Madame would plaster the walls of that cave we
had just visited.  It would not take long to level
those rocks under the arch.

It would take no time at all, I assured him
swiftly, for they would not be touched.   His
eyebrows shot up into the quiff of hair neatly
plastered upon his forehead, and only ejaculating,
" *Comme Madame voudra*," in the tone of one
pitying the mad foibles of an Englishwoman,
but politely refraining from criticising them, he
followed us to the next cave, hotly pursued by
the Italian family.

Here an even stronger odour hit us in the face
as we entered, soon explained by the presence of
the family goat.  The ex-baby rushed in ahead
of us and caressed its ugly head.  This cave was
square in form and, save for its rugged stone walls
and another larger and even more beautiful
circular stone trough at its entrance, unremarkable.
But there was an aperture at the back of it, leading
apparently into the Black Hole of Calcutta, which
stirred our curiosity.

Again lighting his candle, Dante preceded us
into this sinister-looking hole.

" Old Froissart's bedroom," he informed us in
French, at which Mademoiselle and I gaped in
unison and the Italian family guffawed.  " This

was his half of the cottage, and he preferred to
sleep here," went on the mason.

It had no light or ventilation of any kind save
what filtered through the narrow hole through
which we had just crept, and its rock walls were
sweating with damp. But what riveted our attention at once was a curious pointed niche cut out
of the rock in the centre of the back wall. The
interior of this niche was blackened as though by
soot, and underneath it was an enormous circular
slab of roughly hewn stone.

"What on earth is that?" whispered Mademoiselle.

"*On dirait un tombeau,*" remarked Dante in a
sepulchral tone.

"Or is it an ancient sacrificial stone?" I suggested. "Perhaps a torch had been lit in that
niche."

"It easily might be," said Mademoiselle excitedly; "you see, there are several cave dwellings
near here, and on the next property there is a
mysterious blocked tunnel leading no one knows
where, because no one has the courage to risk
gas fumes if it is reopened. Perhaps all these
cave dwellings communicated with each other at
one time. We must get an archæologist to come
and see this place."

In any case this cave seemed an eerie choice of

a bedroom, but quite in keeping with the hardly (though sometimes) human Froissart.

"Madame will, of course, keep her wine and her oil in here when I have cleaned and prepared it," suggested Dante cheerfully, dismissing ghosts of the Provençal past and bringing us back to the practical present.

There remained still another cave which we decided must contain the central heating stove and the coal supply, and in it I discovered a fourth stone trough—the largest of all, oblong in shape, and so massive that it looked as though it could never be removed elsewhere.

"Four of them; did you notice?" I whispered to Mademoiselle, whose only response was another cautionary dig in the ribs and a wink of the eye farthest from the Italian family.

"Now we must climb the slope by the great basin and inspect those ruinous sheds in the courtyard," she announced, leading the way.

"The line of them is so lovely; that sweeping slope of roof," I remarked. "Can't we somehow keep it?"

"You can have a loggia there," decided Mademoiselle swiftly. "It will be perfect for meals out-of-doors in summer because it's on the north-west side with the basin below it. You will have shade and always hear that cool sound of running water."

At this moment appeared Asunta, who had panted up from the Château below to inform us that if we did not descend at once the *gnocchi* that she had prepared for us would be ruined. She stood, flapping her spotless white apron at us as though we were naughty children, making a delicious picture as she stood there in the sunlight, her apricot skin flushed with exercise, her abundance of smooth white hair, and her amber eyes glowing. But we are all terrified of Asunta, and we appreciate her wonderful *gnocchi*, and so we bade a hurried farewell to Dante, disengaged our legs from the clasp of young Italians, called the dogs, and prepared to descend.

" *Bon appetit, Mesdames,*" Dante called after us.

" *Merci—et vous le même. À demain,*" I answered.

" *Biscottes ! Biscottes !* " screamed the ex-baby, toddling hopefully down the path after us, and I looked back to see the whole family of limpets staring at our retreating figures through the vine pergola outside the kitchen door.

# CHAPTER III.

## DANTE IN THE INFERNO.

I HAD empowered Dante to seek out a small army of local masons and boys to help him take off and heighten the roof of the cottage. Once this was done there would be shelter from the autumn rains which, owing to the interminable delay caused by the wily old Froissart, would soon be upon us.

The roof completed, most of the workmen could be dismissed, and the rebuilding of the interior could be accomplished gradually by Dante and one or two helpers.

The dear Domaine, where " Monsieur " and I had lived so happily, was still unsold, so that I should be able to take from it such furniture as I required for the new home, furnish it by degrees as each room was finished, and leave the surplus to be sold with the house.

I had realised that if the Domaine did sell suddenly, before I had found and acquired a new property, I should be faced by the agony of tem-

porary homelessness and the expense of storing
furniture that I might never need, and, as everyone knows, it is impossible to judge exactly what
one will require in a new house before trying
effects.

All this had decided me to secure my old cottage
at once, before selling the Domaine, though I could
ill afford to have two properties on my hands.
Also, I knew that whilst the Domaine was still
mine, I could steal (from myself) cuttings and
plants from its profusion to beautify my new
garden. So my decision was saner than it
seemed.

Very early, the day after our inspection of the
cottage with Dante, I was awakened at the Château
where Mademoiselle was harbouring me, by
rumbling sounds, the metallic clinking of pick-
axes upon masonry, and distant thuds. Throwing
on my dressing - gown I rushed unceremoni-
ously into Mademoiselle's room crying, " It has
BEGUN ! " " What has begun ? The revolution ? "
she inquired, shaken suddenly out of sleep—for
there had been rumours of this danger in France.
" They're pulling down my cottage," I explained
breathlessly. " Oh, is that all," she replied
unsympathetically. " You nearly frightened me
to death," and she irritably pulled the bedclothes
over her head with a gesture of dismissal, while

Squibs, who generally loves me, growled drowsily from the end of the bed.

A bowl of hot coffee hastily swallowed and I climbed the mountain munching my toasted roll, impatient to see how much of my cottage would still remain. For Dante had warned me that the work of demolition was always tricky and that once one began to pull down bits of old houses one never quite knew what would happen. Supporting walls which at first seemed solid, often collapsed or began to crumble when the structure they were holding up was pulled down.

At any rate I was happily certain of one thing, that the Italian family, fearing also to be demolished, would by this time have removed themselves and their possessions.

But not at all. The mongrel cur, with his usual joyous bark, heralded my approach, and the whole family rushed to the kitchen door and out into the garden to witness it.

I wished that I were a British seaman, for they are said to command the most varied and expressive vocabulary of expletives, and I needed a flood of them to relieve my feelings at that moment.

Ignoring the Italians as far as possible, for an effort to be polite was beyond me, I went into the cottage, pursued first by the ex-baby yell-

ing, "*Biscottes! Biscottes!*"—the mongrel cur
nuzzling my hurrying knees and, of course, inevitably by the whole family.

The masons were hard at work demolishing the
roof, and the beaming face of Dante peered down
at me through a great hole above the kitchen
where several young Italians started scrambling
over heaps of *débris* and screaming with excitement.

I was in an agony lest stones should fall upon
their heads, and tried vainly to explain this danger
to their mother, who merely smiled amiably and
pursued me into the next room. Constantly the
masons were obliged to stop work as the baby
or the ex-baby crawled over the heap of rafters
and plaster just fallen from above. It was all
very dangerous and perfectly maddening.

Presently Mademoiselle appeared with Squibs
and Tucker at her heels. The two dogs were, of
course, thrilled by the prospect of a cat hunt, for
the family cat was also still in residence and was
soon nosed out. There followed a wild chase,
the two dogs yelping with excitement, tearing
through the rooms in chase, leaping through gaping
windows, scuttling down stone stairways, terrifying
the children who yelled in chorus, and stopping
all work, for the masons, of course, must see the
outcome of the adventure, and one and all downed

tools and scrambled to some vantage point to witness the finish.

The cat shot through the loft and out on to the roof, where it leaped upon the ledge of a squat chimney. Squibs, to our horror, followed it, sliding and slipping upon the tiles and barking hysterically until her attention was diverted by the sudden appearance of two pigeons, which, scared by the uproar from the loft where they had taken refuge, fluttered through a hole in the roof almost in her face. She then started another *danse macabre* on the parapet, almost giving us heart disease lest she slip and fall into the courtyard.

The frantic commands shouted to her from below, by me, were unheeded, as were the prayers and entreaties of her mistress, uttered cajolingly from the loft. But at last Mademoiselle daringly slithered down the sloping roof and succeeded in quietly seizing Squibs from behind and dragging her into a place of safety.

Tucker, who is large and fat, and who owing to her woolly face cannot see very well, had been blunderbussing round the kitchen, overturning pails and babies and planks whilst roaring at the top of her voice. The mongrel cur sat in the courtyard and howled in unison with the children.

At length all dogs were secured, the cur with his chain outside the kitchen door, and Squibs and Tucker on their respective leads.

Once more we were frustrated in our intention to make serious decisions as to the rebuilding and rearrangement of my new home, and, despairingly, we were towed back to the Château by the excited dogs.

I sent for Madame Pagini at last, intending to implore her and her husband to use their influence to rid us at once of the insufferable nuisance her relatives had become, and to remind her of her solemn promise that the moment I took possession of the cottage they should vacate it.

She appeared during the afternoon, a transformed woman. There was a new air of assurance about her since she had become a capitalist. She had discarded that awful hat, and her scanty hair looked as if it had been washed and waved. She wore leather shoes instead of her squashy black *pantoufles*.

I was quite frightened by her new majesty, and much relieved when it suddenly dropped from her, and, in response to my invitation to sit, she plumped down upon a stool of plaited straw, wiped her brow, and confided to me that she and her husband had gone under cover of darkness, with the purchase money of the cottage safely tied up in a handkerchief, to the house of their *patron* whose land they farmed. He understood business, and they had asked his advice as to what they should do with their newly acquired fortune. He had advised them to put it in a bank, but in such a manner that they could get it out without difficulty whenever wanted. Accordingly, they had all gone together to the bank of his choice, and the Monsieur who owned the bank had given her and her husband each a little book, with pink pages, and told her that whenever she required any money, all that she had to do was to write the quantity on one of the pages and then tear it out, and either bring it or send it to him. (As neither she nor her husband could read or write, I wondered how the signing of these cheques was to be achieved.) It was a beautiful place where all that money was kept, she told me in an awed voice; with a clean white marble floor, and half-way across it were several cages with gentlemen inside them, and the *Directeur* had himself shown her to which cage she must go when she wanted money. There was a hole in the wire through which she must poke her pink page, and then the Monsieur in the cage would poke out the money to her. It was all very easy when once it had been explained; and everyone inside the bank had been so polite; and how

kind it was of the *Directeur* himself to take care
of all that money for her.

Her happiness and importance were pathetic,
and I allowed her to pour it over me until at last
she was obliged to pause for breath ; and then I
seized that moment to ask her aid. She promised
it at once, and was extremely indignant that
Madame should be worried by her nephew and his
family.

" *Sont imbéciles,*" she concluded briefly, and
with that statement I could whole-heartedly agree.

She promised me that her husband would speak
at once to his nephew, and that immediately
Madame should be left in peace to enjoy her new
possession. She then graciously bade me farewell, and left me with hope in my heart that Monsieur Pagini would be able to achieve the apparently
impossible.

And he did—partly—achieve it, for on the
morrow I found that the Italian mother and all
the children, save the ex-baby, had been removed.
But the papa greeted me with his vacant grin,
and a hurried tour of the caves assured me that all
the animals were still in residence.

I questioned the man, who told me that the
ex-baby would spend the day with him, but would
sleep in the new home, and that early next day
his wife would return and help him to remove

their possessions. His uncle, Monsieur Pagini, had promised to lend him his mule and cart to transport them to their new dwelling. Benedictions on the head of Monsieur Pagini. I felt more light-hearted as I went to find Dante and to get his report as to the state of the structure as a whole.

It was fairly good. As he had thought, the outer walls were solid and in good condition save in certain places on the weather side where the rain of years had beaten through the mortar and weakened the masonry. These parts must be taken down and built up again.

Would he ever be able to find *old* stones to match those of the existing structure ? I asked anxiously, and he assured me that he could find enough lying about in the property, and that he would mix his mortar with the bright yellow sand (already ordered) found in the bed of the little Saigne River, the rose-coloured sand of Roquefort, and the purplish sand of Gourdon. These, used with river pebbles, would harmonise with the multi-coloured stones of the old cottage.

I blessed the fact that Dante was an Italian, as had been the old *entrepreneur* who enlarged the Domaine ; for Italian masons realise the importance of such details as these in rebuilding and re-enforcing an ancient stone cottage. To my joy, I learned that he had already found and bought on my behalf a supply of old Provençal tiles to replace those broken on the roof. These are becoming increasingly difficult to discover since Americans and English started buying old farmhouses and cottages in Provence ; but luckily for me a peasant farmer was demolishing his old roof and wished to re-cover it, this time with the new vermilion grooved tiles which disfigure all the cheap modern villas that are springing up like toadstools along the Riviera coast. Dante had swiftly pounced upon the discarded ancient tiles ; and so my roof would not be spoiled by modern patchwork.

Mademoiselle now appeared with a clever plan of the house-to-be, drawn professionally to scale. While I engaged the Italian family in conversation, she led Dante out into the garden and showed it to him. Through a paneless window I watched them ; Dante, lips pursed, hands on hip, tumpkin well to the fore, regarded this work of art reverently, nodding his head knowingly as she explained what she wanted, and producing with an important gesture a bundle of estimates for building materials that he had collected for our choice.

Then he re-entered the cottage, and finding four enormous nails on the floor, placed the precious plan on a wall high above the heads of the children and proceeded to hammer one into each corner of the paper with an old boot which looked as though it had once belonged to the Italian papa.

Thenceforth that plan became the Bible of Dante. It was scanned and studied and adored, but never exactly carried out, though he always firmly believed that he was following it faithfully.

We confirmed a few estimates and then Mademoiselle went back to the Château, there to perform her myriad jobs, and I wandered out into the garden to think over what improvements I could make in it.

Jessamine is a very greedy crop, and nearly everyone of English or American nationality buying a peasant property in Provence uproots the jessamine, cultivates the land anew, and then plants roses, flowering shrubs and fruit trees.

I had already been advised to do likewise, but knowing how much this waste of profitable material shocks the Provençaux, I now decided to keep my little jessamine farm and conscientiously to pick and sell the flowers like my peasant neighbours. I wanted to be practical and to make my small property as self-supporting as possible, so that none could reproach the English widow for wasting blossoms that would fetch money from the scent factories just to have the luxury of their perfume for herself.

Of course I should infinitely prefer to have my

terraces always starred with blossom in summer ;
but my gardener assured me that, even if the
flowers were picked daily, I could still enjoy their
fragrance in the very early mornings before they
were stripped from the plants, and after sunset
when the new buds open.  Also he pointed out to
me that there were a certain number of sickly
plants among them which could be uprooted at
once and replaced by anything else that I liked
to put there.

Outside the little future salon, below the stone
platform covered with its pergola of vines, ran a
wide, curved path edged with more vines that
grew up from the first jessamine terrace, half
covering a beautiful fourteen-foot wall, a metre
thick, of great grey boulders built in Provençal
fashion, one upon another without cement, so that
the rain-water from the earth behind it can filter
through the apertures between the stones and
cause no damage to the construction.

There was no means of immediate descent to
this terrace—one was obliged to follow the path
round to the lower level.  I decided to make semi-
circular steps of the same grey boulders in the
bend of the wall, and to dig up the sickly plants
of jessamine and replace them with English roses,
so gaining colour and scent.  Between the rows
of jessamine I would plant tuber-roses.  All would

be in bloom at the same time, and I had a vision of the tall waxy spears of the tuber-roses thrusting up through a sea of white stars, the whiteness relieved by the pink, crimson, and yellow of my English roses. In the walls I would sow white tobacco plants, and wallflowers, then plant a Mexican moonflower to climb up the vine which covered the stone platform, so that its white trumpets should blow blasts of fragrance into my little salon at night.

I would make a narrow border under the wall and in it plant sweet peas, which would look wonderful against the old stones ; double stocks of every pale shade, with an edging of little English pinks (so called because they are white). As I planned all this I was thinking always of " Monsieur " who used to say, " A flower is not really a flower unless it has fragrance." I would plant a garden such as he loved.

Looking up, I was rudely awakened from my dream by the apparition of the Italian papa, stealthily approaching one of the caves with a horribly purposeful knife in his hand.

Murder was about to be committed. Apparently there would be one beast the less to be removed to-morrow,

Swiftly I fled through the olive grove and back to the Château.

# CHAPTER IV.

## PEASANT PANDEMONIUM.

A SQUEALING of affrighted pigs, quacking of ducks, clucking of hens, the mewing of a cat, the yelping of a dog, the excited shrieks of children, the screaming voice of a woman, and the raucous shouts and loud laughter of men greeted my ears as I walked up to my cottage next day.

Bedlam had not been let loose ; it was only the *déménagement* of the Italian family, and no music ever sounded sweeter to my ears.

Cautiously and surreptitiously I crept round the house, climbed some scaffolding which I knew would be empty of workmen ; for, of course, they were all helping with the family removal, and, crouched behind a chimney, I witnessed the scene in the courtyard below.

There stood Monsieur Pagini's rickety cart already half loaded with miscellaneous household objects : a dilapidated iron bedstead, two chairs (one without a seat), a stained kitchen table, a bundle of bedding (oh ! what bedding), and trusses of hay. My masons were helping stack in sacks of potatoes, crates of hens, ducks, and rabbits ; the Italian papa was battling with struggling pigs that squealed in terror, much to the amusement of the other helpers who left their various packages to assist in tying the poor beasts' legs with rope and then heaving them upon the bales of straw in the cart.

Two jars of olive oil were then fetched, and several cases of grapes and sacks of vegetables. The children (for they had all come back to see the fun) were lifted in and bestowed in any spaces left vacant, and then their mother remembered that she had left their toilet necessities in the cottage. She rushed back and returned with a small tin basin which she threw into the cart, and a little useful enamelled pot which she swung jauntily by the handle on one of the shafts.

This brilliant idea of hers was immediately copied by her husband, who, unable to place his spraying machine, used for the vines, hung that upon the other shaft, to the great indignation of the patient mule within them, who forthwith began to buck and kick. He had borne as much as he could stand, and was now protesting violently.

The peasant papa cursed, the mamma screamed, the children yelled, and an avalanche of hens and sacks and household goods slid out into the road.

73

After which the mule calmed, and held firmly by Dante, the work of reloading began again. Realising that no one would pay any attention to me or my cottage that morning, I climbed down from my spy-point and left my property unseen.

Well, the cottage would really be empty to-morrow, for all the beasts and birds were apparently safely harvested—or were they? Where was that whiffy goat? I had not seen her in the courtyard.

A week later I learned the identity of the victim who fell under the murderous knife I had seen in the hand of the Italian papa, when Squibs, after frantic scrabblings and shrieks of excitement, disinterred a mangy goatskin from a lower terrace of my garden.

I was thenceforth in full possession of my cottage, or to be strictly accurate, in part possession; for the pair of pigeons belonging to the Italians had refused to be caught and transported with the family. They remained, protesting violently against the intrusion of the masons and doing all they could to hinder the work. Hitherto they had owned the two cottages, nesting where they willed in that ruinous interior, and now they passionately resented being disturbed.

The Italian papa—somehow I had had a suspicion that we had not seen the last of him—

appeared daily to claim his pigeons, and I urged him to catch them as expeditiously as possible and then depart in peace.

During the days that followed I was constantly to see him lumbering in chase of the obstinate birds, climbing olive trees where they were perching, only to see them sail off the branch he had just painfully reached ; crawling up scaffolding to catch them in rear, only to be baffled again.

Dante complained that footmarks seen on the dusty floors each morning proved that someone visited the cottage at night, and my gardener complained of trampled terraces in the garden which he had dug and raked before leaving in the evening. I knew that it was the Italian peasant seeking, ever seeking, and finding not, his elusive pigeons. Somehow they contrived to evade him, and to roost beyond his ken.

He daily badgered me to command my masons to catch his pigeons, or to buy them myself, and he was equally importunate that I should purchase the heap of manure provided by his livestock. I did not want either his pigeons or his manure, and begged him to remove both as soon as possible, for I knew that until this was accomplished I should have the pleasure of his company every day until nightfall. One day, however, there was peace. The manure had been removed

75

and the pigeons had apparently left the house and found some refuge out-of-doors.

I resolved to spend most of my time there also, making a garden. In this way I should always be near the cottage to see that Dante carried out the architectural plan of Mademoiselle and to supervise the way in which he did it, while I sowed seeds and planted shrubs with my young gardener during intervals.

I had engaged him when old Hilaire left me— a very good-looking young peasant with not much brain, but plenty of goodwill and enthusiasm. I engaged him because, when I questioned him as to his previous experience, he looked at me with reproachful blue eyes and merely said : *"Il faut avoir le jardin là, Madame,"* placing his hand over the region of the heart.

I felt that this was so right that I engaged him at once, for it is perfectly true that unless one really loves one's garden one will never have any great success with it.

Antonio, for that was his name, proved to me early that he kept the garden in his heart, for he slaved lovingly to beautify it. The work was arduous, for first of all we had to clean it, and for days we removed and unearthed broken bottles and crockery, old tins, old boots, rabbit-skins, decayed bones, every variety of rubbish which had either been interred or else thrown among the bushes by that untidy Italian family.

Then we had to cart away barrow-loads of stones from the surface of the earth before we could dig and manure it. And when Antonio started digging he nearly always struck solid rock before he had dug a foot below the earth. Time and again he tried to dig a hole in which to plant a shrub, then came upon obstructing rock ; and I began to think that my garden would prove to be like that of an American friend of mine who bought a villa on the coast and who told me later that whenever she wanted to plant a geranium she was obliged to blast a hole in the rock with dynamite.

I asked Antonio where I could procure dynamite, and if it was very expensive ; whereupon he launched out upon his very interesting experiences when digging wells in Provence ; the hacking and heaving of great rocks ; the mines he had to explode ; and of one very unpleasant moment he had whilst working at the bottom of a dry well when his pickaxe, dislodging a great rock, unloosed the hidden spring beneath it and water roared forth swiftly, reaching his chin.

Fortunately his comrades rescued my Antonio, and now, once again, he was valiantly battling with subterranean rocks.

We found one lovely pocket of soil just outside my future kitchen, and Mademoiselle, the practical, who had climbed our mountain to see how we were all getting on, immediately counselled me to make a parsley plot.

" Plant in it everything that Emilia will need constantly for her cooking. Parsley, mint, sage, chervil, chives, basilique, and tiny spring onions, and she will bless you every day," she advised me.

This we did, sowing seeds of sweet-william around our plot to form a nice cottagey frill of colour, and a counter-smell to the chives and onions.

I spent one happy morning doing foolish things. I planted a forget-me-not inside the hollow split of an olive tree. I filled a hole in the stonework of the cottage with wet mud and poked a yellow wallflower into it (thereby, later, causing a bad patch of damp on the inner wall of my little guest-room). I sowed nasturtium seeds in an old saucepan and frying-pan left by the Italian peasants upon the ledge of the stone basin. With joy I braced up the pair of ancient boned stays which had once encased the form of the Italian mamma and now encircled the stem of a vine—put there, I suppose, to prevent the supporting wire from cutting into its bark ; and I lodged more firmly the exploded *espadrille* which I found wedged between the fig tree in the courtyard and the wall.

Then I fetched Dante and told him on no account to remove the old kitchen knife stuck in a crevice of the cottage wall from which a clothes-line was suspended, the other end attached to the bole of an umbrella lime tree outside the kitchen ; nor the spiked end of a pickaxe from which hung a battered lantern. I toured the cottage and grounds with Mademoiselle finding like treasures : a tiny battered shovel with a long crooked handle ; an iron ladle which had been bent and hammered to form a *veilleuse* lamp ; and a queer pewter candle-stick. All these would form appropriate furniture for my ancient fireplaces.

I had a lovely time.

Squibs adored my new property. Every morning at the Château she pranced and curveted around my legs, imploring by gesture and the pleading gaze of sherry-coloured eyes, to be taken up to the cottage where new excitement and sport were ever to be found. There was the mongrel cur of the peasants ; there was the half-wild cat ; there were lizards hiding in the crevices of rocks, and those quaint cousins of lizards which look like tiny grey crocodiles and flee up the walls of houses ; there were chameleons and grass-snakes sometimes amid the scrub which covered the lower terraces of the olive grove ; there were rats, mice, chickens, and pigeons to be hunted and chivvied in the cottage, where there was also a marvellous assortment of smells for sensitive nostrils to sniff.

The only disconcerting thing about Squibs is that when the sport becomes keenest she insists that we must share it whatever else we happen to be doing. When we hear a certain hysterical note in her bark we know that she is calling us urgently to come and join in the hunt. There is an obstructing rock to be removed, or someone must poke behind a piece of furniture with a long bamboo to dislodge hidden quarry. If Squibs misses that quarry she will mourn for the rest of the day, immobile near the spot from whence that rat, mouse, or lizard escaped her. Every inch of that lovely graceful little body is sporting and keen.

Once, when I had to go to Paris for a course of treatment, Mademoiselle insisted upon coming too, to take care of me. The problem then became —what to do about Squibs ?

Poor little Squibs—a real country sheep-dog— is terrified of towns. She trembles and slavers at the mouth the moment she approaches traffic, houses, and noise. Yet she really suffers more if Mademoiselle leaves her at home, and once, having been shut into her mistress's bedroom, someone entering after Mademoiselle's departure found Squibs balancing precariously upon a window-sill, just about to jump out of a window twenty feet above the ground to go in search of her mistress. Mercifully the person who had entered the room had the sense to say nothing, but merely crawled silently on all fours up to the window and was just in time to seize poor little Squibs from behind before she took that fatal leap.

On another occasion, I suppose through the negligence of a servant, she contrived to escape from the house and went in pursuit of her mistress's car. After long hours of search she was found, dusty and exhausted, tearing along the main road to Nice, whither Mademoiselle had gone.

How she had escaped being run over by one of the myriad cars which roar along the level and swirl round mountain bends will never be known, but I like to think that the Divine Shepherd looks after His wandering sheep-dogs as well as His errant sheep.

These agonising experiences decided Mademoiselle once and for all never to leave Squibs behind when she went away, and so we resolved to take the little thing with us to Paris.

We waited until the train had steamed into

the station before we went on to the platform,
and then we hurried the trembling Squibs into
our sleeping-car. To avoid having to leave her
alone there while we had dinner in the dining-
car, we had packed up our supper—and hers—
in a basket, and we all shared it happily together.
When she had eaten and had satisfied herself
that there were no rats nor mice in any corner
of our compartment, she became calmer, and later
curled up at the foot of the lower bunk where
Mademoiselle was installed while I climbed up
to the upper one. Suddenly Squibs became restless, peered out, put her front feet on the rungs
of the ladder, and gave a series of short, sharp
barks.

"You've disappeared. She's anxious about
you," explained Mademoiselle immediately. "She
hasn't rounded you up for the night. I must
lift her up and let her see for herself that you are
really up there in your pen."

So little Squibs was helped up the ladder and
scrambled on to my bunk, where she crawled up
to my head, nuzzled in my neck, and laughed in
my face. Then, reassured that I was safely
tucked between the sheets, she waggled that
ridiculous little bob of a tail with a tufty curl on
its end, and asked to be lifted down. And after
that we all went to sleep.

But, arrived in Paris, our troubles began anew because, although we led Squibs to dark alleys and to unfrequented paths of public gardens, she utterly refused to obey the calls of Nature—and Nature must have been yelling and shouting by the evening of the next day. Always the little dog had run far apart from us for her private purposes, and she evidently considered that it would be both immodest and indecent to perform them when attached to a lead.

Poor Mademoiselle and I squandered our substance on taxi-cabs to drive Squibs to hopeful places where trees and grass were to be found, but always we discovered that prohibition against the liberty of dogs. We even visited the Presbytery of a priest to beg his permission to allow Squibs to roam in the walled garden of a Catholic school, but without success.

And then, at last, a sympathetic dog-owner told us that the only places in Paris where dogs were allowed off the lead were the quays of the Seine, whereupon we at once decided that although the Quai d'Orsay Hotel was more expensive than that of our original choice, we would remove there immediately, and the extra cost of hotel would be covered by the amount we should save on taxi fares.

Once installed there, it was easy to run across

the road with Squibs and let her loose on the quay below, and she soon gained confidence and began her usual rat hunts among the derelict boats, piles of ropes, planks, barrels, and refuse.

On our last day in Paris, ten minutes before our train was due to leave, triumph of triumphs, Squibs actually caught and killed a rat on the quay, to the accompaniment of cheers from excited bargees.

Gallant, sporting, little Squibs. We were so proud of her—and she of herself.

Directly the workmen started re-roofing the cottage, I wrote to our new Bishop of Gibraltar and asked him if, when next he visited the Riviera, he would be kind enough to spare an hour or two to come up to our village to bless my new home and to dedicate a tiny memorial chapel I intended to create. Bishop Nugent Hicks, his predecessor, had come to bless the Domaine, and I shall always treasure a very lovely memory of his visit.

Our new Bishop wrote to me very charmingly (and in his own hand, which "Monsieur" always said was the greatest courtesy a busy man could confer upon anyone) to tell me that he would be in Cannes in February. He booked, provisionally, a date for me and hoped that no urgent and unforeseen duties might arise in the meantime to prevent his visit. He told me that by some strange coincidence he had been reading the account of the blessing of the Domaine by Bishop Hicks in my book ' Perfume from Provence ' when my letter was brought to him.

I had not expected that he would be visiting the southern French part of his diocese so early in the year, and my masons had not yet removed all the tiles and rotten rafters from the old roof of the cottage, preparatory to rebuilding. Panic seized me that when the Bishop came he would find only the shell of a house to bless.

But his letter decided me at once to concentrate upon the little chapel, now that the pigs had been removed. Cleaning their late habitation would take some time before any alterations could be thought of, and so I immediately asked my gardener to scrape out the litter within the cave and then dig over the earthen floor. When this was accomplished I engaged a boy with a squirt to fire disinfectant in fluid form over the walls for a whole day.

He stayed with us for a week, because the frantic scratching of the dogs after visiting the cottage persuaded me that it would be a good thing to spray the walls and floors of every room without delay.

When I delicately asked Dante if he and his fellow masons were at all troubled by these inhabitants of the cottage, he stared at me in surprise and assured me that neither he nor his friends had noticed anything; the obvious inference being that they were so accustomed to *puces* in their homes that they had ceased to be bitten.

At length the cave was clean, and after a few days' airing interval I begged Dante to start demolishing the ancient ceiling which had already been condemned. It formed the floor of the second kitchen, soon to be the salon, and the kitchen sink drained down into it through the floor, which explained the dark stain of clotted grease we had found defiling the great grey boulders under that wonderful arch.

Dante, all eagerness to begin work upon the chapel, descended the upper terrace and disappeared into the cave, returning a few minutes later with a mysterious air and an intimate smile to inform me that he regretted that he would be unable to start work on the chapel yet awhile.

What had he discovered in the chapel? The Italian papa? When I questioned him, all that he would reply was to invite me to come down and see for myself.

Much intrigued, I followed him into the cave. He lit his *briquet*, and, his face wreathed in smiles, pointed to a recess in the rocks within which I saw the head and the bright eye of a bird. " *Elle a fait le nid là-dedans,"* he whispered. *" Elle a déjà des petits. On ne peut pas la déranger, la pauvre."*

The mother pigeon sitting upon a nest already full of young ! So that was where she had nested. Of course she must not be disturbed until her family could fend for themselves. No Italian mason would start work in that cave whilst she was cosily tucked into that niche, even for a Prince of the Church and the consecration of a chapel. If it was not ready for the Bishop's visit *tant pis.*

Would he be a human Bishop, human enough to understand if, when he came and chanced to find all not quite in readiness, I told him this little story ? I hoped so.

# CHAPTER V.

## LOTUS LAND.

WORK on the chapel having been effectively stopped for the time being, Dante returned to the roof, and, seeing that the masons would be fully occupied for some days to come and would need no direction whilst putting on the tiles, we resolved to escape to the sea for a much-needed rest and change.

For many years Mademoiselle had rented a deserted coastguard station down on the coast in the Var. I had never been taken there, but Mademoiselle now assured me that as we needed perfect peace and solitude to tranquilise our frayed nerves, her coastguard station was the one place left on the coast where these rare blessings could still be found.

" It's all very primitive down there," she warned me. " No running water, it must be fetched from a well on the shore ; no electric light—only candles and lanterns ; camp beds, lumpy mattresses ; no road to approach the place, only a rather terrible cliff track. Could you bear it ? "

This description might have discouraged me somewhat had I not seen a glow that I had learned to understand at the back of her eyes. Modern comforts might be lacking, but there were evidently compensations which I was to be left to find for myself on arrival.

Mademoiselle now retired to the lovely secret garden of the Château, which ages ago had been a monastery, and there, sitting on the brink of her great swinmimg pool, paper and pencil in hand, she became absorbed in the making of lists. The provisioning of the coastguard station, she informed me, was always a serious matter because it lay sixteen kilometres from the nearest village-town and no tradesmen could approach it. She therefore sent the heavy luggage, cases of food, mineral waters, and sometimes extra camp beds and bedding ahead to St Tropez by car, there to be shipped into a fishing boat and transported to the little Bay of Good Hope, on the shore of which her cottages stood. Passengers and dogs followed in her five-horse-power Baby Peugeot car whose lorryback held an extraordinary amount of baggage. This tiny car could travel along the narrow track on top of the rock cliffs and negotiate its bends in safety with an experienced driver at the wheel.

"You can't take a lot of luggage, you know," said Mademoiselle to me as she emerged from the garden, "because when you get there you'll only have one chair in your bedroom, a store-box for your dressing-table, and a nail hammered into the wall and the rungs of a ladder on which to hang your clothes. Of course you can stretch a rope across the room if you want more accommodation."

"What clothes *shall* I want?" I inquired.

"A fisherman's jersey and trousers, an oilskin and sou'wester, high rubber boots and sand-shoes, a swimming suit, a large sun hat, and a change of underclothing — that outfit provides for all weathers," she answered briefly. "I'll lend you a *musette*—the French soldier's knapsack—if you like, and you can sling it over your shoulder to walk up the shore. Oh! and don't forget your accordion."

I had bought one some time ago, chiefly because the Provençaux love it so and also because it is an instrument, unlike a violin, that needs no accompaniment, and, unlike a piano, can be carried on the back.

Our departure next day rather resembled the *déménagement* of the Italian family. The little Peugeot was so stacked up with curious gear and provisions, not to mention Mademoiselle, myself and Squibs, and Tucker who was coming with us while her mistress was in England.

The little car, in spite of its load, mounted the long ascent of the Esterels mountains slowly but steadily. I sat with my long legs hunched up and Tucker's fat form wedged between me and the door. Tucker is loving, and at intervals turned her great woolly head and snuffled my cheek ; she also made several attempts to leap out of the car when she saw a dog whose appearance happened to displease her. Squibs was tucked under the left arm of Mademoiselle, who was at the wheel, and she, also, had to be restrained from jumping over the door if she scented a rabbit—or saw a cat. So the journey was not without excitement.

We lunched in a pinewood bordering a lonely road, and the dogs had a marvellous hunt for rabbits. Mademoiselle thought it would be a good thing to let them work off some of their exuberant restlessness before we reached that tricky cliff track leading to the coastguard station.

At length we began to climb once more, steeper and more steep became the road, but the gallant little car roared steadily up the mountains in first gear, negotiated a formidable hairpin bend and snorted on to the level of a plateau where the road suddenly dwindled into a rutty cart track with great troughs of hard-baked mud on either side and here and there a bank of it across our path.

"Now you see why I wouldn't allow you to bring the Fiat," shouted the chauffeuse, driving slowly and ever more slowly until we merely crawled.

"This cart track becomes a rushing torrent in winter when the rains come down and swell the natural springs into flood," she informed me. "A friend of mine who took a farmhouse in this valley got stuck in the middle of the stream with her car one dark night. She jumped out of it, waded through the flood, and got home, leaving the car to be extricated in the morning. But next day when she went back to this place with a band of fishermen, the car had completely disappeared. It had been washed right down the valley and nearly into the sea. Cushions and tools were actually found on the beach."

Evidently the winter storms of this region were as violent as those Atlantic gales in Devon which "Monsieur" so often described to me, and I remembered a story told me by a niece of his who then lived on Dartmoor.

One day she set forth in her new Baby Austin car, which was laden with several hundreds of eggs from her poultry farm, intending to sell them in a neighbouring market town.

A terrific gale was blowing great guns and the little car rocked and swayed as she drove, but being well weighted with herself, her two young sons, and the large quantity of eggs, she felt quite safe.

As they reached the summit of a high tor she remembered that a farmer's wife in the valley below was very ill, and she decided to scramble down the hill with the two boys to inquire how the poor woman was, take her some eggs, and try to cheer her up.

This they accordingly did, leaving the car on the top of the tor.

When they returned half an hour later the car had vanished. It had been blown away and was discovered at the bottom of the valley on the other side of the hill, smashed beyond hope of repair and inside it the most glorious uncooked omelette ever seen or imagined.

I told Mademoiselle this story as her little car lurched and bumped over every obstacle ; a wonderful little car.

At last we came to a pinewood, and between the russet trunks I saw a dazzling shimmer of blue that could only be the sea.

"We are just coming to the cliff," warned the driver, " so brace your nerves."

They needed bracing ; for when we had driven

through the pinewood the track narrowed to a mere stony path flanked on one side by mountain rock and on the other—a drop sheer into the sea.

" Light me a cigarette before we reach the bend at the top," said Mademoiselle quietly, and I lit one and put it between her lips. It was then that I realised that the bend ahead of us was the worst part of the drive.

We ground our way slowly upwards, lurching sickeningly over loose stones, scraping the brushwood of the mountain on one side and leaving a margin of about a foot on the side of the sea. Before us the path seemed to end abruptly in the sky.

I set my teeth and shut my eyes, wondering if the end would be painful or swift, and I opened them again a few moments later at the sound of stifled laughter. The car had stopped. We had rounded the bend in safety.

" Oh, if you could only have seen your own face," wheezed Mademoiselle; " I'm sure you thought your last hour was come, and, with that awful imagination of yours, were seeing us all maimed and broken on the rocks below, perhaps waiting for hours—even days—before some fisherman found our damaged bodies. Was I a brute to make you face this road ? But now—look below you. There are the cottages down on the shore."

I looked . . . and the sheer beauty of what I saw left me speechless.

Below us lay a perfect little sand-fringed bay flanked on one side by great grey rocks between which grew clumps of umbrella pines, and on the other by a huge rocky peninsular—almost an island. Between these barriers a lovely valley ran inland carpeted with wild white alyssum and sea-lavender and bordered by pinewoods.

At the sea-end of the valley, built upon the sand-dunes above the bay, was a long low line of whitewashed, red-roofed, one-storeyed cottages —the coastguard station.

And this picture was semicircled by a hoop of sparkling sea. What a sea ! That marvellous Mediterranean blazed and scintillated as though some alchemist had thrown all the sapphires, emeralds, turquoises, aquamarines, crystals, and amethysts in the world into one great crucible and transmuted them into fiery fluid. There were tones of sapphire and emerald over the deep water ; turquoise and aquamarine above hidden strips of sand ; amethyst where lay concealed great rocks ; sparkling crystal where the sun touched the ripples.

At length I looked at Mademoiselle.

" Well ? Do you like it ? Is it at all what you imagined ? " she asked me, smiling softly.

" It is impossible to imagine the impossible,"
I answered. " This place can't be real—I'm just
dreaming."

" I hope you'll be able to dream to-night on
your camp bed," she retorted practically. " We
had better go down and inspect our mattresses,
which are probably damp as well as lumpy, unless
Marius has had the sense to drag them out into
the sun when he got my letter."

" Marius ? "

" Oh, Marius is my man-of-all-work when I come
down here. He's the son of a fisherman and a
dear," Mademoiselle informed me. " I wonder
when the boat will come with our provisions."

At that moment a sailing boat rounded the
rocks and came into the little bay.

" There it is," exclaimed Mademoiselle in the
tone of a General satisfied with his staff work.
" They've timed their arrival well."

" Or perhaps *you* timed it ? " I suggested.

We drove down the cliff and over the hard
sand to the garage shed at the end of the row of
cottages, and while Mademoiselle, having given
me the keys to open them, strolled down to the
shore to greet the fishermen, I had time to explore
by myself.

The end cottage formed a communal kitchen.
It had a great open fireplace and a charcoal

brazier, a larder cupboard, an ancient stone sink, and even a tiny *glacière* in which by some miracle ice is made by lighting a paraffin lamp underneath.

This was the one touch of modernity ; the rest of the interior was as primitive as the blackened beams above my head from which were slung strings of russet onions and fishing-tackle. A ladder led up to a wooden railed-in gallery where once the fishermen had stored their nets.

The other cottages—I visited each in turn— were built upon the same plan. Each had a deep-walled recess for a bed and another, alongside, as a dressing-room, with a gallery roofing them above with a ladder to climb up to it. Each had its great open fireplace, its window back and front, and its own front door opening out into a kind of sand-floored *patio* shaded by plaited bamboos, so that each occupant of each cottage, though joined to its neighbour, was entirely private and independent.

The cosiness of it !

" Which cottage have you chosen ? " inquired the voice of Mademoiselle behind me. " I should advise the one nearest to the kitchen ; then, if it rains, you won't have so far to splash forth for your food. Well, now that you've made your tour of inspection, what about lighting some fires for us while I unpack the stores ? "

" I'd love to," I assented eagerly, " but where do I find wood and all things necessary ? "

" You'll find plenty of driftwood on the shore and dry branches and pine-cones in the woods, and some sacks in the garage," she informed me, and I felt a helpless kind of fool to have asked such a question in such a place.

" Take Squibs and Tucker with you," she called after my retreating form.

I called the dogs, who came tearing after me, yelping and barking with excitement, rolling on the sand-dunes, worrying at each other in mimic battle, leaping up at me and seizing my empty sacks in their teeth, then scurrying ahead of me to the shore.

Tucker, to my amazement, rushed straight into the sea up to her armpits. It was a hot day and she, clad in her heavy fur coat, was breathless after her exertions. She stood, her great woolly head just above water, panting in ecstasy. Squibs, sighting a seagull, tore along the sand and over the rocks in futile chase screaming with excitement, while I wandered about picking up driftwood and sprigs of red and white coral, climbing rocks and peering into deep pools.

So clear was the water that I could see vivid weeds and moss, sea-urchins, shells, and coloured pebbles lying on their bed of golden sand, and the

flash and glitter of small silver fish as they darted
through the still pools among the rocks. So
fascinated was I that I quite forgot what I was
supposed to be doing until a cry of, " Hi ! What
about the fires ? " recalled me to my duties, and
I left that wonderful sea and ran towards the
woods to pick up pine-cones.

When I got back to the cottages I found the
fishermen who had brought our stores helping
Mademoiselle to beat mattresses and put things
in order. They were all old friends of hers and,
while hauling in packing-cases and fetching water
from the ancient well, told her the news of St
Tropez, where she possessed a studio. Then,
when all was made cosy and habitable, fires lit
and beds made, they squatted on the sand of the
*patio* and drank her health in the Château wine.

The most restful thing about Provence is the
fact that no one is ever in a hurry. There is a
lovely leisure in the lives of the Provençaux ;
if a thing can't be done to-day there is always
tomorrow, so why hurry ? *Demain—ou après-
demain*—and this is very soothing, especially to
one who is always " fighting fire," as Mademoiselle
says I do. She says my energy exhausts her.
" Relax ; oh, do RELAX," she constantly implores me.

Here, in this Paradise of a place, with no sound
save the murmur of the sea and the sigh of the

wind, this should be easy, I thought, as I gazed dreamily at the loveliness around me.

Our fishermen, having presented us with some delicious fresh fish for our supper, bade us farewell at last and climbed into their boat, promising to tell any of their friends who might be fishing in that locality during the next few days, to come ashore and share their catch with us.

I shall always remember those lovely late September days of sunshine, so hot that we lived in our swimming suits, running in and out of that glorious sea in the intervals of grilling fish over our charcoal brazier and doing our various household chores. After sunset when the temperature suddenly dropped several degrees, we lit roaring fires of driftwood and wrote or read by the light of candle-lanterns, or, while Mademoiselle cooked our supper, I played to her on my accordion to the accompaniment of melancholy howls from the dogs (are they howls of ecstasy or suffering I often wonder ?).

Every day Marius appeared, sauntering over the cliff path clad in blue fisherman's slacks, a *béret* pulled over one ear, and a scarlet handkerchief knotted around his throat. Generally he carried a bunch of flowers from his mother's garden, and always he was whistling. He whistled as he fetched water from the well and afterwards sloshed it over our brick floors or washed up the dishes. He whistled as he peeled vegetables for the dogs' soup, laid the fires, created a writing-table for me of a store-case and wood picked up on the shore, and he whistled loudest of all as he selected a spot commanding the loveliest point of view whereon he intended to build for us an outside inconvenience on the site of an old Saracen tomb.

Before we left I learned all the Italian and French love songs popular at the moment, for Marius knew them all. He was a treasure of a man-of-all-work, spoke little, worked ceaselessly, and whistled much.

Save for Marius we saw only the postman, who, when he considered that enough letters had accumulated to make the perilous ride along the cliff path worth risking, appeared on a bicycle; and an occasional fisherman, who hailed us at dawn and left us some fresh fish.

The peace of it was so perfect. No masons to supervise, no Italian papa to evade, no domestic problems to solve, no eternal questions to answer. We could rise early or late and go to bed when we pleased ; have breakfast at luncheon-time and lunch at tea-time if we so desired. We forgot the date of the month, the day of the week, and the hour of the day. Nothing mattered.

We rambled about the mountains and woods

collecting pine-cones and wood for our fires, while the dogs madly hunted for rabbits ; we fished for sea-urchins in the deeper rock pools with a long bamboo, one end split into three and a cork pushed between these prongs to hold them open. We caught *pulpi* (baby octopus which are very good fried) ; we prised limpets off rocks ; we bathed at all hours of the day, and once by night in a phosphorescent sea clothed only with blue fire.

I could never be sure whether the little Bay of Good Hope were lovelier by day, when the surrounding sea dazzled one with its brilliance and myriad colours, or by moonlight, when the pine-clad mountains stood smudged dark against a starry sky and a path of silver led across the water to the majestic pile of rocks.

The solitude and quiet of that place were so wonderful, broken only at night by the occasional muffled roar of an aeroplane, the throb of a distant liner, or the voice of a fisherman singing an Italian love-song as he speared fish attracted to his boat by an incandescent flare.

This form of fishing fascinated me. I would come out of the kitchen and see the white bows of a boat brilliantly illumined by the flare above them, the dark form of a fisherman standing with poised spear ready to harpoon the fish, which, attracted and dazzled by the pool of fire around them, became his easy victims. Really a form of poaching ; but very picturesque poaching.

I began to dread the rare arrivals of the one-armed postman lest he should bring me a summons to return. Dante had promised to let me know when the re-roofing of my cottage was completed and it was time to cope with architectural problems, but now, in this lotus land, I had begun to wonder why I had bothered to build a house with bathrooms, electric light, and every modern comfort when I could be so divinely happy in a fisherman's rough cottage with none of these things.

Really I suppose we buy houses in which to store our possessions, then we must insure them and engage servants to guard and care for them. How much happier we should be if we could carry all that we possessed in a knapsack on our backs.

I aired these views one night to Mademoiselle, who was inclined to agree with me.

" If there was a revolution in France and the mob came to pillage the Château, and we had to flee, which of your possessions would you want to save ? " I asked her.

She smiled, and after a short pause for reflection began to count them on her fingers. Only three fingers were required and she had done. And not one of the things she wished to keep had anything but a sentimental value. My list was equally short.

"All the same, you'd miss your great library of books, and, if you lived in this cottage always, you'd feel cramped after a time and you'd long for a hot bath with water, h. and c., gushing automatically from taps, and food that appeared ready cooked," teased Mademoiselle. "Oh, I think you'll enjoy the comforts of civilisation after life at the coastguard station."

"Perhaps you're right," I sighed. "But this is a heavenly existence."

## CHAPTER VI.

### NICOLAS.

OUR heavenly existence was marred the very next day by an accident when Mademoiselle slipped on a seaweedy rock and injured her foot.

"I must go to Nicolas," she muttered when the pain had a little abated.

"Who is Nicolas?" I asked. "A doctor?"

"No, he's a fisherman—but he's rather extra-ordinary," she answered. "I can't explain him, but you'll see for yourself if you'll drive me there. It isn't far from here; a little fishing village farther along the coast."

Marius helped us to start the Baby Peugeot by pushing her downhill like a child's perambulator. Having negotiated that dreadful bend on the cliff pathway, which, however, was far less terrifying when mounting from the coastguard station, we turned along a lovely inland road which wound through pungent pinewoods (no one who has smelt that aromatic resin under a southern sun can ever forget it) across a line of mountains with, at intervals, a glorious view of wooded valley and bordering sea.

Then the road twisted farther inland and we drove through valleys where the peasants were all busy with their *vendange*, the women picking clusters of purple grapes and filling baskets which the men loaded into cases and then into carts. Everyone we met was stained purple and in joyous mood ; the men sang and joked with each other as they worked ; some of the girls were crowned with vine-leaves, and all the children were gobbling grapes. We waved to them gaily, and they waved back.

We turned a bend of the road, passed between thickets of bamboo, swept past a strip of wooded beach, and approached a lovely little secret bay dotted with fishing boats and fringed with small white cottages.

" Here we are," said Mademoiselle. " Nicolas has his name painted in large blue letters on his cottage and so you can't miss it," and soon I saw through a gap in the pine trees the little house we sought. Drawn up before it was a peasant's cart.

We left the car at the side of the road, walked through the pinewood, and followed a little path leading past a neat line of allotments to the cottage. Just as we reached it, two men were lifting out the prostrate figure of a man from the cart. They looked at us anxiously as we approached, and one of them asked us if we had an appointment with Nicolas. Whilst helping with the *vendange* their friend had fallen from a lorry and injured his back and his leg. He was in great pain—perhaps he would never walk again. They had heard that Nicolas could surely help him, and so they had borrowed this cart from a neighbouring farm and had brought their *camarade* at once. If we had immediate need of Nicolas they would wait. . . . The man they were carrying looked at us with eyes that pleaded for our patience.

"Take him in at once," said Mademoiselle, "I am in no hurry. There is nothing in the least important the matter with me."

They thanked her gratefully and began a painful ascent up the steps of the cottage. The wounded man was heavy and they could not avoid hurting him as they moved.

Suddenly, from the back of the cottage, appeared a man clad in a blue vest and loose linen trousers. Two pigeons perched upon his shoulders and two dogs and a cat followed close at his heels.

"There's Nicolas," exclaimed Mademoiselle softly.

I saw a burly, thick-set man of middle age, with a ruddy, clean-shaven face in which were set a pair of amber eyes. It was a strong face, striking in no particular save for its expression of kindness and compassion.

On seeing the pathetic efforts of the men with their limp, helpless burden, it creased with concern. He shooed away the pigeons, dismissed the dogs and cat with a swift caress, and strode forward to support the poor sagging body. With his strong help the ascent was quickly made.

"*Doucement—doucement*," he enjoined the men. "*Courage!*" he heartened the sufferer. Then, catching sight of Mademoiselle, his whole face lit up and he gave her a little reassuring nod before they disappeared into the cottage. A moment later he put his head round the door to tell her that he had expected her that afternoon, and had remained at home. In a few minutes he would be at her service.

"Expected you?" I asked in surprise as the head of Nicolas disappeared. "How could he have known that you were coming?"

"There is a great deal about Nicolas that can't be explained," said Mademoiselle. "I told you that he was rather extraordinary. Once I came here without making an appointment and his wife told me that Nicolas had gone out and would not return till late that night. I was terribly discouraged because I had hurt my shoulder and it is a long way from here to the Château. Suddenly a voice behind me said, ' I felt that Mademoiselle had need of me and so I came back.' And there was Nicolas."

A rosy woman hanging out the family washing in a garden near-by looked at us with friendly interest as we sat on a bank, smoking cigarettes, and asked us if we had come to see Nicolas.

" He is a good man, Nicolas," she said. " My husband was out of work for eight months and while he was lifting a heavy weight he hurt himself badly. Nicolas tended him for weeks until he was cured, knowing that we could not pay. He helps all the unemployed, who come to him from far."

An old man came down the path and the woman greeted him over the hedge. " I was telling these ladies how Nicolas cured my husband," she told him.

" *Ah ! c'est un brave homme, Nicolas,*" nodded the old man, his face aglow with enthusiasm. " He came to my farm in the night and saved my best cow."

" Is he a doctor ? What does he do ? " I asked her, since Mademoiselle would not attempt to explain Nicolas to me.

" I cannot tell you, Madame," the woman replied. " It is his touch—he finds out the ill and then he takes it away. One cannot explain it; it is a gift of the good God. Madame will see for herself."

Mademoiselle smiled secretly as she nursed her injured ankle, then she looked up at me quizzically and said—

"What a woman you are for definitions. You always want complete descriptions of everybody; I suppose it is so that you can have a picture of them in your mind. Well, one can't describe Nicolas. Madame must wait and see for herself," she concluded mockingly.

At this moment the door of the cottage opened and, to my infinite amazement, I saw the injured man hobble forth leaning on a stick, his face beaming with delight. He descended the steps very slowly but obviously without pain, followed by the two peasants who had carried him in. Awe and astonishment were expressed almost ludicrously by their staring eyes and dropped jaws as they watched their *blessé* walk down those steps without their aid. Nicolas himself stood upon the top step, laughing happily.

"*Ca va mieux, eh?*" he called after him, and the man joyously shouted back, "*Je comprends!*"

Then Nicolas turned to Mademoiselle, apologising for having kept her waiting. She introduced me; my hand was enclosed in two muscular paws and I was assured that any friend of Mademoiselle's would always be welcome in his cottage.

He led us into the quaintest room that I have ever seen, and while he went away to wash his hands in the kitchen sink (I saw him doing it with energy through the half-open door) I had time to look around me.

The walls were covered by a terrible wallpaper, a mauve background with mustard-yellow stripes and medallions enclosing bouquets of red roses tied with blue ribbon. There was a small open fireplace in which sputtered three lighted pine branches, and before it lay a cosy cat, fast asleep. Above the mantelpiece was a tarnished mirror in a gilt frame, and beneath it were placed highly coloured china vases packed close with massed zinnias, asters, and a few late roses, a wonderfully gay clash of colour, deliciously cottagey.

On the walls were hung enlarged photographs ; a portly picture of Nicolas with his gun and two dogs ; two wooden-faced portraits of an elderly man and woman, certainly parents of his ; an army *citation* of the *croix de guerre ;* a peculiar device for telling the weather—a mechanical monk who appeared to have feasted upon much rich food, pointing with his staff to wind, rain, or sunshine marked upon an obelisk ; and a bracket holding a stuffed owl with wings outspread.

The furniture consisted of a plain divan covered with cheap towels, a wooden chair, and a table upon which lay a tiny open pill-box of tin, containing, apparently, talcum powder.

But the ceiling was best of all. I had not noticed it at first until Mademoiselle called my attention to it.

" Isn't it divine ? " she said. " A Russian peasant painted it in gratitude to Nicolas for free treatment. Don't you adore those cows kicking up their heels in that corner ? " Each corner was decorated with active beasts or birds. Two cocks fighting, two cows trying to jump over the moon, a cat with arched back confronted a bristling dog, and two horses galloping over a field. Each of these pictures was enclosed in a golden hoop. In the centre of the ceiling painted lambs frisked around an electric bulb.

We were still both lost in admiration when Nicolas reappeared. " You like my beasts ? " he asked us, smiling proudly. " I thought they would cheer my *malheureux* when they come to me for help. They lie on that divan and look up at familiar country sights. It changes their ideas."

" And that poor man ? " asked Mademoiselle, " he looked dying when they carried him in, and he walked out without help."

" Oh, it was nothing," he replied quickly,

" only muscles and nerves displaced in his back. After I had arranged it, of course, he could walk. And now, Mademoiselle—that foot."

She sat down upon the divan, and, having first dusted his hands with powder from the pill-box, he knelt before her and passed his hands lightly from knee to ankle. When he touched the injured part there was a startling crackling sound as from an electric contact, and Nicolas drew away his hands with an exclamation of pain. After a moment he resumed his curious, unconventional massage, and every time he touched an injured muscle or nerve-centre there was this same crackling sound. His face became beaded with sweat.

" Crrrrrrrrrrrrrrrrraaackkk ! " he tried to imitate the sound. " Do you hear it, Madame ? " he said, turning to me ; " every time I find a sick place there is that craacckk in my fingers and I take the ill from Mademoiselle. I feel it all in my arms and down to my toes. *Diable !* there is enough of it."

I watched him very closely, thinking at first that he made this curious sound by snapping his fingers, but I saw that they were always rigid and that he massaged with the ball of the hand and the fingers pressed together. Perfectly extraordinary.

" Does it hurt ? " I asked Mademoiselle.

"Not in the least," she replied. "That is the wonderful part of Nicolas's treatment, it is absolutely painless—except to him."

He found more trouble in the calf of the leg and under the knee, but at length he sat back on his heels, and with the exclamation "*Ca y est!*" beamed up at Mademoiselle.

"Now move your leg and foot in any way," he insisted. "It will not hurt you any more. I have arranged it."

Obediently she turned it this way and that without, as she assured us, a twinge of pain.

"Only muscles and nerves twisted and displaced," he assured her; "if you had broken bones I should have had to send you to *Monsieur le Docteur.*"

"When did you first find out that you had this wonderful gift?" I asked.

"When I was five years old I handled a maimed puppy and found that I could cure him. And then I tried to help my schoolmates when they hurt themselves."

"But how do you know what is wrong?" I persisted.

"The blood and the nerves tell me," he said simply. "I can't explain it. *C'est naturel.*"

He did not appear to like talking about himself and changed the subject by asking Mademoiselle if she had had a good harvest of grapes and if she had yet made her wine ; whether there was the prospect of a good olive crop at home ; and they talked on all the country topics dear to both their hearts.

"Have you been very busy this summer, Nicolas ? " she asked at length.

" There are always my *malheureux*," he answered. " Between the seasons there is not much work and *sous* are scarce. When they need help they come to me. And there have been many visitors to the south this year, Americans and English, staying in hotels all along the coast ; they send their cars to fetch me in the mornings, for in the afternoons I must be here to tend my *malheureux* who come to me on the four o'clock train."

The little spuffle-train which fussed past below our Domaine three times a day, to the perpetual amusement of " Monsieur," who would peer out of his *Galerie* window, eyeglass in eye, and then report with a chuckle, " One peasant in it to-day, Sweetheart," as he watched it snorting and puffing up the mountain.

Once I had asked an official why the little spuffle-train was not discontinued since no one seemed to use it, but I was told that one day it might be useful " to rush troops up to the frontier " —RUSH troops up to the frontier !

Its local name was *la pomme-de-pin*, and Hilaire, our old gardener, explained to me that it was so called because it rolled slowly down the mountain like a pine-cone. Whereupon Emilia, our little *bonne*, instantly contradicted him and said that the train had gained that name because it went so slowly that it would be possible to jump out, gather up a basket of pine-cones, and then catch it up again farther along the line.

I realised that this was the same little spuffle-train to which Nicolas referred, and though it descended nearly empty from the mountains, apparently when it reached the coast it picked up a cargo of peasants.

My thoughts, so apt to flicker and fly back to " Monsieur " and the little Domaine, were recalled by a roar of laughter from Nicolas. " We ate WELL, I can tell you, Mademoiselle," he was saying. " He was generous, *ce type*. He had a bad arm and so he sent his car to fetch me, and gave his chauffeur orders to feed me on the journey, and—we fed. They gave us *langouste*, hot, with rice and a tomato sauce ; and after that a bird, and cheese, and fruit. And we shared a bottle of good wine." He patted a tumpkin already beginning to be a little too large for a man of middle age.

" Nicolas," warned Mademoiselle, " you are getting fat."

" Hit me, Mademoiselle," he urged indignantly ; " that is muscle. I am hard all over, it is not fat."

All the same, it was quite evident that Nicolas was a *bon viveur*, liked his food, and knew how it should be cooked. He enjoined me to eat red beef-steaks grilled for a moment or two over vine clippings to give them a flavour, because he thought me too pale.

" I had one of such beauty to-day," he told me. "A poor girl was brought to me this morning who had not been able to open her mouth for more than an inch since she was a child, so had hardly spoken a word for years and had to be fed on liquids. Then, yesterday, she had a violent tooth-ache and went to the dentist, who, of course, could do nothing for her since she could not open her mouth. The man of teeth sent her to me, and I found the jaw displaced and arranged it for her. And then—she talked and talked and talked, and nothing could stop her talking until I told her that now she could go away and eat a beef-steak. She was wild with excitement, and I took her and her mother to the *café* here and she devoured her first enormous meal of solid food.

" It did me good to watch *la pauvre petite* eat her *déjeuner*," he laughed. " *Figurez-vous, Madame*, for her it was a new sensation." His part of the story was not emphasised at all, only the delight of the poor girl who could at last eat and talk normally.

There was something immediately lovable about Nicolas. He was like a happy boy, and his simplicity and *joie de vivre* were so refreshing.

"And now, Mademoiselle," he said, turning to her, "you can run and jump as before."

She got up and walked easily to the door.

"Thank you, Nicolas," she said, "it doesn't hurt any more, and I am grateful, for my feet are useful to me. Can I use them to walk round your garden ? I want to see if your vegetables are as good as mine." She prides herself upon her *primeurs*, being a scientific gardener.

She walked out of the cottage and down the steps without even a limp, and Nicolas and I followed.

"*Elle est brave, elle,*" he said to me, "*brave et simple.*" The highest compliment a peasant can pay and, I thought, the one most to be desired.

On the way back to the coastguard station Mademoiselle was able to drive the car, for which I was thankful as I frankly funked that last cliff ascent and that horrible bend. We talked much of Nicolas.

"What a perfectly extraordinary natural gift he has," I said ; "how do you account for it ?

Is it electricity ? I noticed that before he touched your foot he stretched out his arms as though he were gathering something from the atmosphere. It was quite an unconscious gesture, but I wondered."

" I don't know. I can't tell you," she answered.

' There are more things in Heaven and Earth . . .' I thought ; and there have been wise men and wise women, sorcerers, white witches and black witches, magicians, charmers, and healers all over the world since Time began. Probably people with some strange magnetic power, some inborn instinct, some natural gift, or stronger will-power than their fellows.

" Provence is full of men and women like Nicolas," said Mademoiselle. " In nearly every village and town there is a wise man or woman who really has a power of healing, or of putting right displacements. There's an old woman in Grasse, very nearly blind, whom Asunta swears by, and whenever she hurts herself I have to send the car for *la bonne femme*."

Then I remembered that once when poor old Hilaire had a touch of the sun he came to me and asked permission to go home. I asked him if he would let me telephone for our doctor, but he refused me gratefully and said he knew exactly what to do. When I pressed him, he sheepishly admitted that there was *une bonne femme* who could take away sunstrokes, and he meant to visit her. He did, and next day was at work again as well as ever.

"When I was very ill, long ago," Mademoiselle told me, "the peasants of the village swore that an old mad woman who had haunted my property, stealing vegetables, chickens, &c., until I warned her off, had put a curse on me. One of them persuaded Asunta to take a garment that I had worn to a certain wise man who could then lift the curse. I believe he boiled it under a new moon, muttered certain incantations over it, stretched it for several nights upon dew-wet grass, and did other mysterious things. I did get better, but I probably should have in any case. The Provençaux are frightfully superstitious, and, of course, there are plenty of charlatans who trade upon that superstition.

"But Nicolas is perfectly genuine. A very well-known Parisian specialist who was sent down here to rest and live in the sun because he had something wrong inside him, and was killing himself with overwork, heard of Nicolas, and drove down here some time ago with the purpose of unveiling a charlatan. He made no appointment, but just walked into the cottage, and Nicolas, thinking that he had come for help, immediately diagnosed his mysterious malady. Since when that doctor has sent his patients to Nicolas when their symptoms baffle him, and he's not the only doctor I know who does that.

" Then there was a writer living near Grasse whose eyes were troubling him. Each oculist he visited suggested some new treatment. He went to Nicolas, who discovered congestion in the head and displaced nerves, gave him that curious massage, and now the eyes are quite well.

" I sent a poor workman who was supposed to have a tuberculous spine to Nicolas, who found displacements of muscles and nerves around the spine, and now the man is walking. I could go on. One can't account for that gift of his, but it exists all the same.

" The nicest thing about Nicolas is that the success he has never spoils him. He remains a simple fisherman, going out in his boat at night, and tending his vines, his garden and his *malheureux* by day, perfectly happy and content.

" Quite lately a rich American offered him a car so that he could visit distant hotels along the coast, but Nicolas refused it. He said there were so many poor who needed him and if they came to his cottage for help and found it empty, what would they do ? The rich, he said, could look after themselves, pay for good doctors, or, if they wanted Nicolas, they could drive to his cottage. I love that in Nicolas. He really does want to help humanity at large. His wife told me that if someone in the village is ill in the night, Nicolas, with that extraordinary instinct of his, *feels* it and cannot rest. He gets up and goes out to find them and see if he can help. They all adore him here." . . . . . . . . . . .

After all, the twelve disciples were but simple fishermen.

# CHAPTER VII.

## RUDE AWAKENING.

TUCKER and I were having a bathe, passively and actively. She was content to lie submerged in a shallow rock pool, her shaggy head just above water, one of her quaint habits perhaps learned from her boon companion Dulcibella, the duck.

Dulcibella was hatched in an incubator, one of only three survivors, for Mademoiselle in her pioneer days of poultry raising had not yet learned that ducks' eggs and hens' eggs require different temperatures. A quantity of each had been placed together in the incubator, and the ducks' eggs suffered in consequence.

From the beginning Dulcibella proved different from her two companions. She was not a gregarious duck, and, in her effort to obtain solitude, she climbed out of the flannel-lined basket wherein all three ducklings were temporarily housed, waddled weakly to the edge of the table whereon it was placed, and—fell dizzily into the void.

Poor little Dulcibella was maimed, but only

123

slightly. She was picked up and placed tenderly inside the woolly jersey of Tucker's mistress, whom she thenceforth adopted as her own, never so happy as when sitting on her shoulder wibbling lovingly with her beak over the neck of that mistress, pulling her hair, pecking softly at the lobes of her ears, and crooning love-songs in a language all her own.

Dulcibella developed a passion for her owner, following her everywhere, screaming in the hall when her mistress mounted stairs too steep for webbed feet to follow.

Out-of-doors it was the same. Dulcibella assisted with gardening operations, eating all the succulent worms turned over by the trowel. If left alone, she protested with loud lament until her mistress returned, when she would hasten down the mountain to meet her, quacking with joy and overbalancing often from excess of speed.

At the moment Dulcibella was visiting the coastguard station, having arrived in a basket with her mistress who had brought her many mountain miles in a car. We had been apprised of their coming by this telegram :—

" Dulcibella has laid her first egg. Bringing her to-morrow for some sea air."

Dulcibella adored the coastguard station and

her new diet ; feeding upon the tiny snails to be found amongst the sea-scrub growing in and around the rocks ; and one *festa* day, gorging herself with locusts when a migratory swarm settled for a few hours upon the sand-dunes.

In the evening her crop was so swollen that she could hardly waddle to her bed—a shallow straw-lined basket in her mistress's room in which every morning she deposited an egg. The duty of the day accomplished, she then visited Mademoiselle and me in our respective cottages, announcing her arrival with loud and cheerful quacks.

To my astonishment neither Tucker nor Squibs resented the presence of Dulcibella in any way. One would have imagined that Tucker might have been jealous of the devotion of this duck to her mistress, and of the extreme possessiveness of this devotion which sometimes took the form of sharp pecks at attainable portions of Tucker's anatomy if she ventured to approach her owner when Dulcibella was near.

But no, Tucker's attitude towards the duck was one of amused toleration ; and Squibs at once included it as one of the sheep for which she was responsible and rounded it up at night when she went her usual round to see if each and all of us were safely in our pens. After which, with a gusty sigh, her work for the day accomplished, she would leap upon the bed of Mademoiselle, there to remain, curled up at its foot, until morning.

To-day I was swimming around in the hot sunshine, when, warned by the furious barking of Squibs who was guarding the cottages and her mistress, and the violent quacking of Dulcibella who was waddling about in the *patio*, I espied the postman descending the cliff path on his bicycle.

I swam ashore, and, hurrying into my *peignoir*, ran up the shore, waddled after by a roaring Tucker. Both she and Squibs detest bicycles.

Several letters and newspapers had accumulated since the postman's last visit, and among mine I found an envelope addressed to

### Madame de Fortec

in a sprawly, illiterate hand.

It was from Dante, our little Italian mason, and it pulled me out of the dreamy atmosphere of lotus land with a jerk. The roof of my cottage was finished, he informed me, but as Madame was amusing herself well by the sea, and certainly would not wish to return immediately, he proposed starting work on the partition wall inside, following his own design which he enclosed for me to see. If my hair had not been damp with sea-water it would have stood on end.

This was the design :—

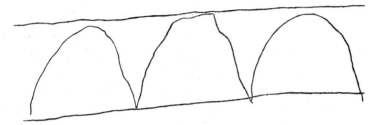

Laughing helplessly, I handed it to my architect. " There's no time to be lost," she exclaimed. " He'll DO it if we don't hurry home. I only gave him a rough plan for the size of the rooms with no details of the interior. Think of three pretentious Provençal arches leading from one kitchen to the other, when there ought only to be one simple square opening. Why on earth can't the man go on working on the outside walls which must be patched up in places ? "

" But don't you love his design ? " I asked her. " Can't you see him drawing it at home in the evening, and Madame Dante admiring his genius ? "

" I can see your cottage being wrecked if we don't go home at once," she answered. " We'd better begin packing up, and Marius can load up the car when he comes."

I could not help realising that she was right, although my heart was heavy at the thought of leaving the peace of the coastguard station, and I said so.

" It is only a few days earlier than we intended to leave it, anyway," she strove to console me, " and you do feel rested and more able to cope with things at home, don't you ? "

Although somewhat unkempt of appearance we were both looking and feeling enormously better. We no longer frowned fiercely when asked a simple question, nor paused for a perceptible time before we could concentrate our thoughts enough to answer it ; and when we dropped things we quietly picked them up again instead of merely kicking them. So that our nerves were evidently more tranquil.

" I feel resurrected and rejuvenated," I answered cheerfully, " and as I've got to house my *sacré* possessions somewhere I'd better get a move on with the cottage."

The strain of *La Chalande qui passe* came drifting on the breeze, and Marius, whistling as usual, appeared over the crest of the cliff. It was nice to see his dismayed expression when we told him we must go home at once, for it showed that he regretted our departure. The daily bouquet of flowers had given us an inkling that our inarticulate *homme de menage* liked us ; but his expression now was far more eloquent. At once he asked us if we should be returning soon, and, although I think neither of us believed in our hearts that escape would again be possible for some length of time, we told him that we hoped to come back very soon. That, at least, was true.

We departed from the coastguard station well ' bunched ' (as the Americans say) by Marius, who ran ahead of the car to warn his mother of our going and stripped her garden of flowers for us. Their fragrance, mixed with the odour of fish presented that morning by a friendly fisherman, perfumed our homeward journey.

We had a lovely picnic in the Esterels and reached the Château just before sundown, tired, but happily anticipating a hot bath, and then something delicious cooked by Asunta. It looked as old as Time, the ancient stone walls bathed in sunset light, the two giant cypresses guarding the secret monastery garden, dark and velvety against a sky of fiery rose and clear pale green.

It all seemed wonderfully peaceful, but appearances can sometimes be deceptive, and, during our homeward drive, Mademoiselle and I had made a catalogue of all the tiresome or worrying things that might possibly have happened in our absence, so as to prepare ourselves in advance to meet them. But it is always the unexpected that comes to pass, we had not anticipated the welcome that we got.

As we entered the courtyard a howling as from the throat of a demented wolf met our ears.

" Heavens ! what is that ? " I asked in consternation.

" I should think Asunta has hurt herself," replied Mademoiselle quietly ; " that is the noise she always makes when in the slightest grief or pain. Few Italian peasants have courage, you know."

" *Santa Maria ! Christ !* " shrieked the invisible sufferer.

No one answered our summoning ring at the front door, and so Mademoiselle rapped thunderously with the massive iron ring suspended upon it since monastic days, and, although the howling never ceased for a moment, after a time we heard the sound of flapping *pantoufles* within, and an affrighted eye rolled at us through the *grille* in the top panel.

It was the eye of Beppino, Asunta's young son, who, assured that it was his mistress who desired to enter, opened the door and stood pallid and dishevelled before us.

His mother had a bad finger, he told us breathlessly, and *Monsieur le Docteur* was just cutting it off. He, Beppino, had been hiding in a cupboard to muffle the sound of *maman's* screams. No, she was not alone. Her daughters had come, and the washerwoman was also with her.

"I must go upstairs at once and see what it is all about," said Mademoiselle wearily to me. "Will you tell Beppo where to unload the things from the car."

She came down later, white and exhausted, to tell me that poor old Asunta had a whitlow under the finger-nail. She still had her finger, but it had been lanced in three places by the doctor. "She really did have something to howl about this time, poor old dear," said Mademoiselle. "It was a sickly business, but she's in less pain now, and when she's calmer I suppose the mourners will descend to the kitchen and have a good meal at my expense—unless, of course, they intend to stay the night."

The two daughters did remain to nurse their mother and to console the unnerved Beppino. The washerwoman departed after a good square meal, and it was very late before we got ours, cooked up somehow by one of Asunta's loquacious daughters.

Next morning, the second-born knocked at the *salon* door while we were having breakfast to inform us that her sister had a very bad sore throat, and had spent a feverish night ; it was certainly *la grippe*. *Maman*, however, felt better this morning.

We were just about to start an epidemic of influenza.

Both of Asunta's daughters went down with it, and, finally, Asunta herself. The Château became a nursing home, with Mademoiselle as nursing matron, until she herself was stricken on the same day that poor old Asunta developed phlebitis.

I became nurse, housekeeper, housemaid, and sometimes cook, assisted by the beautiful but sloppy Beppino. It was a dreary and weary time, rendered hectic for me by the necessity of climbing the mountain daily to my cottage to superintend Dante and his angels. Luckily we returned in time to avert those three grisly arches, and the pigeons having hatched out their young, I was able to deflect his attention to the tiny chapel. But I dreaded the moment when he would be ready to begin work on the ceiling, for my architect had decided long since that it must be slightly vaulted and had her own very definite ideas on the subject. Now she was in bed with an obstinate temperature, and I know nothing whatever about architectural proportions. Although I can appreciate beauty of building and discern defects I do not possess the technical knowledge to correct them, nor did Dante ; so I kept him at work on the walls and hoped that Mademoiselle would recover in time to design that ceiling, for I wanted my chapel to be the loveliest thing of all.

In spite of agitations and anxieties at the Château, I had one rather brilliant brain-wave. Dante insisted that I must put in an apparatus of central heating in the chapel as, on two sides, it is below the level of the earth and, otherwise, would always be damp. I was aghast at the idea of an iron tubular construction inside a primitive chapel, for I had decided to leave the walls of rugged boulders just as they were and to pave the earthen floor with stone.

And then it suddenly occurred to me that we could put the radiator in the neighbouring cave (which would one day be my pantry) and knock out a stone or two in the ancient partition wall so that the heat could filter invisibly through these rough fissures.

I may say now that this was done with complete success, and it always delights me when visitors exclaim upon the warmth of my little chapel and search vainly for its source.

Mademoiselle did recover enough to be able to design the ceiling. I can see her now, looking rather like a half-fledged bird, all eyes and beak, bending a long bamboo and holding it up to form an arc from corner to centre, and Dante, eyes on stalks and mouth pursed into a little red circle, following her line as faithfully as he knew how with plaster and trowel.

The result is quite beautiful, and no one will believe that the gracefully vaulted ceiling is of more recent date than the ancient walls.

The furnishing of the chapel now became urgent if it were to be ready for the Bishop early in February. Our influenza epidemic had lasted some weeks, and the November rains frequently stopped all work. Luckily the roof was on, and a certain amount could be done indoors, though the autumn gales, roaring and whistling through gaping doors and paneless windows, drove the rain into the house and made a morass outside the cottage. The few workmen that now remained would start strengthening an outside wall in full sunshine; then suddenly great indigo clouds would descend upon the mountains, and a wailing wind brought the inevitable deluge. The men would strive to continue working, their heads and shoulders draped with sacks, but soon it would become impossible to mix the mortar, and they all sludged home in the mud.

I had been through all this before when "Monsieur" and I were enlarging our Domaine, and for that reason the delays caused first by the vacillations of old Froissart and then by persistently nesting pigeons had so exasperated me. I

had been keenly anxious for the work on the cottage
to be well advanced before the bad weather
set in, but, thanks to that tiresome old man, we
had lost two months of southern sunshine.

The only thing that I could now do was to
think out my scheme for the furnishing and
interior decoration of my new home, and, as the
Bishop was coming to bless it early in February,
I must first start my search for the fittings of the
chapel.

Somehow, somewhere, I must find a few ancient
wooden benches, and, most important of all, an
altar to stand in the recess under that wonderful
arch. I had thought of either a massive block
of oak, supported at each end upon boulders, or
a mighty slab of stone. But I would keep an open
mind and an open eye.

Then Mademoiselle told me of two clever people,
a Frenchman and a Russian lady who had an
antique shop in St Tropez. They drove all over
Provence in a rattletrap car and unearthed
treasures of every description. Their energy and
enterprise were, she said, unbounded and their
prices very reasonable. They sounded just the
couple for me.

" You know I still have a studio in St Tropez,"
she informed me. " I arranged the loft of a
fisherman's cottage overlooking the old port, and

I sometimes go down there to work. I look after myself and do my own cooking. We might go down there for a few days and you can hunt round that shop and see what you can find. A breath of sea air may blow away our microbes, and since poor old Asunta must go home and rest her leg for a bit, housekeeping will be easier in that little place."

"Would it be possible for us to go to-morrow?" I asked eagerly.

"Anything is possible if you really want to do it," she answered.

"I'll go and make arrangements at once."

# CHAPTER VIII.

## THE OLD PORT OF ST TROPEZ.

I HAD only seen St Tropez in summer, and then only the ' wicked ' part of it. Someone had taken me to one of the restaurants (once a mere cave where fishermen had housed their boats, nets, and barrels of wine) bordering the new port. We had arrived at the *apéritif* hour, when semi-nude modernity in all its forms invaded the place to drink cocktails. Its arrival was heralded by a chorus of shrieking klaxons, as great cars came snorting into the town, covered with these curious creatures (seen only in the south of France, and they must be seen to be believed). They overflowed the seats inside, squatted on the bonnets, and balanced themselves on the running-boards. They assaulted the quiet town with their arrogant possessiveness. They perched upon the restaurant tables and shouted for their favourite drinks.

The *apéritif* hour during the summer season is supposed to be ' one of the sights.' It certainly proved to be that, but, although very far from a prude, I had not been amused. It hurt me, somehow, to see the simple fisher-lads standing apart and watching all this with eyes half hungry, half resentful. It made me feel a little sick, and soon I pleaded a headache, and was driven home.

Some time afterwards I was talking of the Var to a strange Englishman who was my neighbour at a luncheon party, and he asked me if I knew St Tropez. I answered shortly that I did.

" What did you think of the fauna of that part of the world ? " he asked me.

" Weird and wonderful," I replied briefly.

He looked astonished and said, " Well, I saw scarcely anything remarkable when I was there."

I stared at him and retorted, " Well, go to the new port at the *apéritif* hour next time you visit St Tropez and you'll see a great variety."

Whereupon he, in his turn, stared at me, and then suddenly burst out laughing.

" That's very good," he chuckled ; " I was speaking seriously, though. I'm a naturalist by profession."

I now gave Mademoiselle my impressions of St Tropez, and she looked at me with great sorrowful eyes.

" I know. It's awful," she admitted sadly ; " but I am going to take you to the fishermen's quarter above the *old* port. That, thank heaven, is still unspoiled. We'll go there to-morrow."

We went, and the moment we drove under the ancient stone archway leading to the fishermen's quarter I was transported centuries back. The narrow street was so roughly paved that at first I feared that all my tyres were punctured, so shattering were the bumps as we ascended. The mud-guards almost scraped the walls of houses on either side, and constantly we had to stop so that fishermen might, by rushing up doorsteps, avoid being crushed, and women, mending nets outside their homes, might draw their chairs indoors to allow us to pass.

At length we reached an open space on a low cliff, and here we left the car, shouldered our knapsacks, and proceeded for the rest of the way on foot.

" Here we are," suddenly ejaculated Mademoiselle as we entered a steep alley, edged by white cottages, with a glimpse of sea beyond the old roofs below.

We descended the narrow path, pausing at intervals to admire the adorable little improvised gardens flanking each doorstep. Pots of vivid geraniums, sedums, and ferns, banked in with barriers of lichen-grown cork ; pale blue ' morning-glory ' convolvulus clambering up white walls and overhanging beamed lintels ; great white shells stuck endwise into green-painted corks.

"Condici, my landlord, is a Corsican ; nearly all the fishermen here are Corsican. He is *très brave*, really, although he has an awful temper and occasionally drinks and beats his wife," explained Mademoiselle. "I found this place fifteen years ago and arranged the top floor as a studio with a communicating bathroom ; and on the floor below I have another bedroom, a small living-room, and tiny kitchen. They now consider me as a member of the family, and Monsieur Condici told me the other day that he had bought a plot of ground in the cemetery as a family burying-place and had left a little space for me."

They very evidently did consider her as a member of the family, for the moment they heard Squibs's familiar bark as she chased one of the many cats around us flying up the alley, the whole Condici family flowed forth from the cottage in a torrent and fell upon Mademoiselle. Her hand was wrung by a swarthy man whom I took to be her landlord, her cheeks were kissed by the women, and her knees embraced by the children. Never have I heard such a joyful din of welcome.

I, as her friend, was warmly accepted at once, and together we jostled into the house *en masse*, and were propelled up the stairs to her kitchen, where a fire was burning, and flowers, in jam-pots, had been arranged to give us welcome. A smell of fish pervaded the cottage, and Madame Condici proudly displayed a great bowl of *bouillabaisse* which she had cooked for our supper. The family remained with us, talking and laughing while we unpacked our stores and possessions, and Mademoiselle produced the toys she had brought for the children.

We were both tired from the twisty drive over the Esterels, but it was impossible to dismiss these simple people. However, at last, doubtless torn away by pangs of hunger, for it was past their usual supper-time, they bade us *au revoir* and clattered down the stairs to their own rooms on the ground-floor.

"Now I will show you my studio," said Mademoiselle, and we climbed a narrow stairway, lit by an old ship's lantern, and entered a great quiet room with simple whitewashed walls decorated only by a few bold sketches of her own, and plain wooden shelves upon which stood trees of coral, a curious shell or two, and some models of ships, one delicious one inside a bottle. The furniture was old but of the simplest and plainest, as used by the fishermen. An easel, a divan-bed, and an open fireplace in which roared a great fire, completed the room. With her usual perfect

141

taste, Mademoiselle had understood the spirit of the place and kept it unsullied. No wonder these fisher-folk gave her their respect and devotion.

The most striking feature of that studio was its view. One end of the room was formed almost entirely of glass : two huge windows and a glass-paned door leading out on to a stone balcony, literally overhanging the sea. Standing upon it one looked from right to left along the Gulf of St Tropez, bordered by distant mountains, and directly beneath lay the ancient port flanked by crazy old houses and a rough stone jetty protecting the tiny harbour with its strong arm. Along this pier, or platform, rusty red nets are usually stretched out to dry, and beside it are moored small fishing boats. But no words could adequately describe the colour of that scene : the blue and violet of the distant mountains, the hot blues and clear vivid greens of the sea ; the russet and ochre of old tiled roofs, nets, and sails ; and the gaudy hues of the orange and scarlet handkerchiefs tied around heads, throats, or waists of copper-coloured fishermen.

We were not destined to sleep much that night, for our bed-going was late, and hardly had we sunk into tired slumber when we were awakened by an appalling clatter. Mademoiselle had insisted that I should occupy the divan in her studio while she slept in the little room on the floor below, and I heard her leaping upstairs as I leaped out of bed and opened the shutters of the window overlooking the alley at the back of the house.

By the light of an ancient hanging lantern we saw a procession of *pubelles* (rubbish pails) rolling down the incline to the little square below, pursued by the unsteady figure of a fisherman. As we looked, he kicked over yet another standing outside our doorway. Something had evidently annoyed him at home and he was venting his displeasure in this delightful way.

I had always longed to do things like that myself when irritated, and envied clowns in music-halls who threw plates and dishes about until the floor was strewn with broken crockery. But *pubelles* now seemed to me to be far more satisfactory, for, instead of a mere solitary crash when overturned, they continued to clatter and rumble and clash as they rolled about, spilling squashed tomatoes, coffee grounds, potato peelings, fish-heads, and egg-shells in their headlong career.

Above the enraged man, on both sides of the alley, we saw shutters being stealthily pushed outwards and windows softly opened ; and then, reflected upon opposite walls, we saw intimate

143

household scenes silhouetted in shadow against oblongs and squares of light.

A window opened next to ours, and we saw reflected a line of garments strung across a kitchen to dry. Shadows from a ghostly fire danced and flickered over them, and the witch-like figure of an old woman stood motionless in the centre of a square of light, listening intently, a frying-pan poised in her hand. Farther along the wall, framed in an oblong, were the heads of a man and a woman pressed close together, evidently peering secretly over the window-sill and making love at the same time. It was like watching scenes thrown upon a sheet by a magic lantern, and we were both entranced.

After a while the door of a cottage at the top of the incline opened, and a young woman came out and followed the reeling form of the man up the alley and out beyond on to the cliff. She returned in a few moments, laughing artificially and murmuring to herself to reassure the neighbours who, she evidently knew, were secretly witnessing her humiliation. Then she re-entered the cottage, shut the door, and presently the strains of an Italian love-song, played upon a cheap gramophone, stole upon the air.

" She's trying to lure him back," whispered Mademoiselle.

" I should prefer him to remain where he was till his head was cooler," I replied.

The ruse succeeded and the man presently returned, entered the cottage, and for a time there was silence.

" Is it over ? " I asked.

" I don't think so—and *they* don't think so," whispered Mademoiselle, pointing to the shadows of those silent watchers. " You'll notice that they haven't shut their windows and are still alert—and look," she said, peering down ; and I saw dark-shawled figures padding into the alley, who then stood motionless in the shadow, staring in the direction of the cottage.

" That innocent-looking cottage has seen tragedy once before," she went on. " One of the daughters of the house fell in love with a French marine. He always came to visit her in her home at the end of each week, and one Saturday, when he didn't turn up, that terrible southern jealousy was aroused, and she walked all through the night to Toulon where he was quartered, found him philandering with another woman, and shot him dead. I don't know what has happened to her, whether, the crime being *un crime passionel*, she was acquitted or whether she is still in some French prison. Anyway, she has never been seen here since, and these people are evidently hoping for another sensation."

Suddenly the stillness was broken by the harsh voice of a man rising higher and higher in drunken abuse, and then by the terrified sobbing of a woman.

The watchers in the alley were galvanised into activity, and a cluster of people, evidently relations, rushed to the cottage and forced open the door. They all entered, closing it behind them, and then from within came the sound of loud voices, louder sobs. Through a dark archway emerged an old woman, her sparse hair shining silver in the moonlight. She stood irresolute, in the middle of the alley, listening tensely, one hand clasped over her mouth. Then taking the pointed ends of her shawl in either hand she flung her arms outward, then forward, folding the shawl tightly over her meagre chest with a wide determined gesture.

"That's the mother of the girl," whispered Mademoiselle. "She has decided that she has the right to interfere."

The old woman hobbled up to the door, but, once there, her movements were arrested by the sudden onslaught of a younger woman who appeared from a dark corner dragging a small girl by the hand. The old woman protested violently in pantomime, but the clinging hands of the two drew her away from the door just before it was violently thrown open and a little party of people stumbled forth, supporting the drunken husband, who was now crying noisily. They led him away, the cottage door closed behind them, and we heard the sound of bolts being shot home as they all vanished down the moonlit alley. Evidently sympathetic relations had offered asylum for the husband until he should be sane and sober enough to respect his wife.

The windows of the neighbouring houses were then softly closed, the shutters latched, and silence once more enveloped the scene.

" That's the end of that," commented Mademoiselle as we shut our window. " Perhaps another tragedy has been averted from that cottage by those silent watchers."

We then each devoured an orange and returned to our beds, but I could not sleep, and when the faint light of coming day filtered through the shutters upon the whitewashed walls, I put on a coat and went out on to the stone balcony to breathe the fresh morning air.

Dawn was stealing softly over the Gulf ; the sky and sea were one pale moonstone ; the drowsy silence stirred only by the sound of little sleepy waves, yawning and stretching on their bed of

sand, and the beautiful hollow note of the cow-
bells tied by the fishermen to their nets to guide
them in the darkness.

The sun, like a fiery eye fringed with gigantic
eyelashes of gold as the rays around it pierced
the morning mist, peered lazily over the rim of
the mountains, and the world began to wake.

Down on the quay the door of a cottage opened,
and a fat Corsican woman came out, stretched her
arms with a wide ungraceful gesture, and gaped
in the morning air. Then she started grumbling
at someone within the house. Next she brought
out a small tin basin containing about a litre of
water, seated herself upon a stumpy chair in the
doorway, and yelled, " *Viens, sale bête !* "

The *sale bête* proved to be a skinny urchin in
the state of nature, who suddenly darted from the
door of the cottage and dashed to the edge of the
quay, hotly pursued by his irate mother, brandish-
ing a towel. He dived into the sea only just in
time, and she stood scolding on the rocks bordering the port while the fishermen, who had begun
to work in the boats, roared with fresh and
boisterous laughter at her defeat. Evidently he
preferred to plunge into an icy sea rather than
submit to the maternal ministrations.

She waddled, muttering, back to the cottage,
entered it, and presently appeared again, dragging

another child, who stood fidgeting while she
scrubbed his face unmercifully with a wisp of
rag, he protesting shrilly against this uncomfortable rite.

In turn the mother scoured her third-born,
fourth-born, and lastly (I hoped), her fifth-born,
a pale and podgy baby, in the communal basin
with the communal rag ; and when they had all
been thus smeared over, she sloshed the murky
contents of the basin with energy across the
paving-stones. Mademoiselle had warned me that
all emptying was done from windows and door-
ways, and that here, in the fishermen's quarter,
one must walk warily.

The family ablutions over, the Corsican mother
entered the cottage, soon to return with a gaudily
coloured mat, which she spread before her door
and plomped the younger children upon it in
turn, where, I supposed, they would be left to
roll about in the sunshine in company with the
various hens, dogs, and cats that pervaded the
port for the rest of the day.

" This evidently fascinates you, as it does me,"
said the voice of Mademoiselle behind me. " But
I think you'd better come in and have your
coffee. It's all ready in the kitchen, and Madame
Condici has grilled us some fresh sardines ; can
you face them for breakfast ? "

149

I could not, but I enjoyed my hot coffee and roll before going out into the little town to explore the antique shop. Its owners were perfectly charming, and immediately grasped what I wanted for my chapel. They would do their very best to find all that was necessary so that it would be ready for the Bishop. I found a lovely long and narrow Spanish table with twisted iron legs, and the frames of some plain Spanish chairs of dark wood, which would do splendidly for my hall dining-room (the larger of the two kitchens, with the great open fireplace backed by boulders). The very sympathetic Russian lady suggested that she should make trellised seats of wide stitched bands of white webbing, which I thought sounded simple and lovely, and I immediately ' fell ' for them. It was a dangerously attractive place, and in the end Mademoiselle urgently dragged me out of temptation.

When we got back to the cottage we were greeted by the sound of a strident German voice shouting in the ground-floor kitchen.

" Monsieur Condici has just bought a wireless set," Mademoiselle explained ; " let's go in and see him."

We entered the Condici kitchen and found Madame cleaning sea - urchins for the family *déjeuner*, and Monsieur seated with his head

actually pressed against the wireless apparatus,
apparently soothed by the deafening din of the
Teutonic voice bawling advertisements for tooth-
powder, boots, motor-oil, and other commodities
into his ear. He looked up at us with a vacant
glare and muttered, " *Moi, je ne comprends pas
un mot.*" Yet he still remained glued to the
apparatus all the time we were talking to his
wife.

During our stay in St Tropez, Mademoiselle and
I decided to cook alternate meals in utter secrecy,
so that we might each prepare for the other surprise dishes. I am far too nervous ever to be a
very good cook. I am too earnest and conscientious over my cooking. I study recipes
from various cookery books, I agonise over details,
and I found it excessively agitating to supervise,
simultaneously, potatoes baking in the ashes of
the open fire of the studio upstairs, the dogs'
soup simmering over the fire in the living-room,
something else roasting in the oven of the tiny
oil-stove, and a sauce heating upon the electric
cooker which had an impish habit of fusing at
critical moments, and had to be repaired by the
light of a candle-end in the most intimate little
room of the flat where the electrician had con-
siderately placed the main.

These reparations, when in the midst of cooking

a meal, are almost as dangerous and trying to the temper as I found leaping over prostrate dogs in the tiny kitchen, when I was at work there. Also, my mind being often full of the subject upon which I am writing, I am apt to forget that the handles of metal saucepans become white-hot if left over a flame ; that raw meat is sometimes full of pipes and elastic, and therefore tough to cut ; and that knives are occasionally sharp. If my meals were fairly successful, I scarcely ever appeared at one of them without bandaged wounds. The food might be ready more or less to time, but the tending of casualties by Mademoiselle delayed its serving. And I must regretfully confess that there were days when, " struck by the splendour of a sudden thought," I seized my writing-block and covered pages of it feverishly while hot food congealed on plates and the toast went up in flames.

Mademoiselle generally cooked the evening meal when daylight had faded and painting became impossible. The streak of genius apparent in all her works appears also in her cooking, and her suppers were *chic*, *recherché*, beautifully presented —and well worth waiting for. She never hurried nor became flustered as I did, but loped lazily about the kitchen, cigarette in mouth, frying-pan in hand, pursued by a circus of adoring dogs.

Sometimes she disappeared to her studio from whence the strains of a negro spirituel, played upon her gramophone, would presently float down the staircase, and I would mildly wonder whether the music were merely beguiling an interval of waiting for something to cook or if she had become suddenly vague, as she often does.

Once, warned by the chimes of the church clock that the hour was late (for we had then no time-piece in the studio), I violated her strict rule that I should never enter the kitchen during the preparation of her meal, and, emboldened by hunger, I poked a diffident head round the door to ask if supper was nearly ready. I found the artistic *chef* absorbed in sculpting a lemon into a human face—eyelids cut in the peel, realistic eyeballs moulded in the glistening fruit beneath, a strip of tomato-skin inset to represent modern lips; and I was told in a dreamy voice that supper had been waiting to be eaten for an hour at least.

Christmas would soon be upon us, and it occurred to me that a clock would be a useful gift to the studio-flat, and, seeing an advertisement of a fine cuckoo-clock, guaranteed to cuck every quarter of an hour, I ordered one from the Parisian advertiser, and asked him to send it to me at this St Tropez address, saying that I would pay for it on delivery. Lest my name should be unknown to the St Tropez postman, I directed the firm to send the clock to me care of Condici, Mademoiselle's landlord.

For days I awaited my parcel, but no clock appeared ; and then one day the fisher-girl whom Mademoiselle had hired to come in and wash dishes and make our beds described a violent scene which had been enacted that morning on the ground-floor—which explained the extra noise we had been hearing. Madame Condici was, we were informed, sodden with tears. A parcel had come addressed to her husband who was expecting some parts for the new wireless set, and she had unsuspectingly paid for the parcel on delivery. When Condici came in he had opened it and found, not the electrical device he had expected, but a miserable little cuckoo-clock.

Was it a joke some enemy had played upon him ? Why had not his wife opened the parcel and verified its contents before paying for it ? He was absolutely furious, and, when furious, always became violent. He had beaten poor Madame Condici hard and hurriedly, and then strode off to the Post Office to get back his money. All he got was a handful of printed claim-forms, which he must fill in and despatch. The officials firmly refused to refund the money, and I imagine that only the solid wooden counter between them and Condici had saved them from being beaten too. The enraged man, being himself unable to read or write, had then made a tour of the town in search of some educated person who could pen menacing threats to the merchant who had sent this idiotic clock unless he took it back immediately and returned the money. The handful of maddening and quite incomprehensible claim-forms were scornfully thrown to an old fishwife in the market to wrap up fish for her customers.

Our ' daily help ' had pieced together this story from the narratives of eye-and-ear witnesses in the Post Office, the fish market, and the streets of St Tropez ; for the whole town was in an uproar, everyone talking of the cuckoo which, in the insolent way of its kind, had forced itself uninvited into the Condici nest.

Mademoiselle and I listened to this story of wrath and tears in the utmost consternation.

" Why on earth didn't Condici come up to us and tell us about it first ? " I said to Mademoiselle. " It ought to have occurred to him that the parcel might be intended for you or for me."

" Because he lost his temper first and beat his wife," she replied. " I have threatened to leave his house for ever if he ill-treated poor little Madame Condici again."

" Well, I'd better go down to him at once and

explain matters," I said hurriedly, " and also see if I can catch my unfortunate cuckoo before it flies back to Paris."

I went down to the Condici kitchen, and there followed a lengthy explanation amid the fumes of frying fish. So violently agitated was Condici that at first I feared that I also should receive a beating. But when, having been told the small sum he had expended upon that unlucky cuckoo (somehow augmented by fifteen francs, though I never inquired into this discrepancy), I produced the money at once, the atmosphere magically cleared, Madame Condici dried her eyes with a dirty dish-cloth, Condici spat upon the floor, narrowly missing my feet, pouched the money, and, after having insisted upon my reading his wonderful letter of remonstrance to the Parisian firm, turned on a blast of Italian opera on his beloved wireless-set to blow me and my cursed clock upstairs.

The tiny cuckoo-clock was found to be packed in several separate parts, which were cleverly pieced and gummed together by Mademoiselle. The finished result—such a minute thing to cause so great an uproar—we hung triumphantly in the kitchen.

Thenceforth, every fifteen minutes, the cuckoo shot forth and uttered a tiny but piercing hoot of derision because the clock gained four hours a day, so that our meals seemed later than ever.

But when the cuckoo informed us that we were lunching at 6 P.M., we had the comforting knowledge that it was really only two o'clock, and that we had, so to speak, four hours in hand.

" I adore your Christmas present to the flat," remarked Mademoiselle when the cuckoo, as was his habit, had interrupted some profound statement of mine with his usual hoot of derision.

" At any rate that cuckoo will always save us from the crime of taking ourselves seriously," I replied. " And talking of Christmas presents, oughtn't we to start making those awful annual lists ? And oughtn't we to go home soon and see how Dante is getting on ? "

# CHAPTER IX.

## CHRISTMAS IN PROVENCE.

DANTE had got on. He had strengthened and patched the outside walls with old stones and mortar mixed with soot and multi-coloured sand, so that the additions were not apparent. He had demolished ceilings within the cottage and re-plastered them. The partition wall between the two old kitchens had been completed, the chapel roof was finished, and the stone-paving had arrived. When the Bishop came in February he would at least find the shell of a house and the site of a garage to bless, and I still had faint hopes that before then I might have found suitable fittings for my chapel.

"I feel that we ought somehow to celebrate Christmas in the cottage," I said to Mademoiselle. "How best can I feast my workmen? What do they like to eat?"

"Game of some kind," she answered. "They love *gibier*, as high as possible; pheasants, partridges—something like that. Get Emilia to cook them at the Domaine and bring them over in a basket. We can heat them up here. She'll like to have a share in the excitement. We can cut the birds in halves so that each man has half, and as they always eat game using only their fingers and teeth, you won't have the bother of supplying knives and forks. After that, oranges, apples, nuts, crackers, cheroots, cigarettes—the usual things; and I will supply them with Château wine."

So I ordered these delicacies in advance.

That being disposed of, we turned our thoughts towards our Christmas lists.

Having lived so long in the little village Mademoiselle has become part of it, and this makes Christmas a season of heavy work for her. There are many poor parents who have learned to expect a fat turkey for the family *déjeuner* from Mademoiselle on Christmas Day, and their children anxiously await that annual basket of toys, never realising all the thought and work they represent.

In every important French town there is a store known as the Monoprix (so called because nothing in it is of the same price). It is supposed to be the French equivalent of Woolworth's Stores in England, but the resemblance lies only in the variety of its stock. Just before Christmas it is packed to suffocation, *bourgeois papas* and *mamans* in search of presents for their families ; the very poor, dragging hungry, wide-eyed children up and down the narrow alleys between the stalls, to feast their eyes and noses upon sights and smells of merchandise that cannot be purchased ; young men and maidens buying cheap trinkets and scarves ; and English and American residents of the neighbourhood choosing toys and ornaments to decorate Christmas trees for their respective villages.

Weary, footsore assistants strive hard to keep their tempers and their heads, a perpetual elastic smile stretching their tired features. They are deafened and dazed by the continual roar of a loudspeaker relaying jazz music from somewhere or other and half-stifled by the atmosphere reeking of cheeses, cheap scent, garlic, peppermints and oranges, and all the mixed goods piled up for sale, dominated by the odour of human exertion ; for it is hard work elbowing one's way laden with parcels through the narrow aisles thronged with a mob of sauntering, lingering, and undecided people.

Amid this pandemonium we did our Christmas shopping.

" Do you think little Germaine would like this ? " asked Mademoiselle, pointing to a miniature kitchen dresser hung with utensils large enough to be used.

" You see she is thirteen now and beyond toys, and it might fire her to try to help that over-worked mother in her kitchen." Every gift she bought was carefully considered, and she never left a stall without a word of sympathy or encouragement to the vendor.

" *Oui, Mademoiselle, c'est tellement fatiguant. Nous sommes épuisées le soir,*" sighed one elderly *vendeuse* plastered against a wall of high-smelling cheeses with the loudspeaker yelling in her ear.

No wonder the poor things were exhausted at night after standing and running about in that atmosphere for hours. We ourselves were in a state of collapse after two hours of it ; but we revived somewhat in the open torch-lit market-place, where oranges, nuts, flowers, and vegetables were piled in profusion under coloured umbrellas to protect them from the unusual rain.

One little Spanish salesman, who was rather sulky at first, thawed into volubility when my companion asked him if his oranges came from Mallorca. It was his island. Did Mademoiselle know it ? Indeed she did, and loved it too. Often she sighed for its little red sausages made of pork and red peppers. The little man was transformed. If Mademoiselle would but wait a moment he had a gift that he would be proud to present to her. He dived into a dark archway, and after a few moments returned with a screw of newspaper which he presented triumphantly to Mademoiselle. In it was the end of a little red Mallorcan sausage.

" We shall eat the other end of it for our supper," he told her excitedly, " and we shall be happy to think that Mademoiselle is sharing it."

How touching these little incidents are—the human side shown only to sympathetic eyes.

In all the smarter shops there was an air of strain. After the collapse of the £ sterling, American and English tourists were few, and the season of Christmas was but a sad affair for the shop-keepers. Their windows glittered with goods that no one could afford to buy, and if one entered timidly to ask a price, one was fallen upon by would-be vendors. Their assortment of articles for sale was not so varied as it is now—the risk was too great to dare to lay in a large stock. " If Madame considers this beautiful object too expensive, prices can always be arranged." A forced gaiety of manner disguising discouragement and real anxiety was assumed by all the *commerçants*, but a word of sympathy and the mask dropped.

" No, Madame, the season has not been good to us—these rumours of wars—the difficult exchange —people do not come to the Riviera for Christmas as they used. This year we cannot afford assistants to help us—you see, only *la famille*—even *la vielle maman* is helping us this year." And there, sure enough, in a sheltered corner, was the poor old mother, muffled up in shawls, her slippered feet upon a footstool, wrapping up a small parcel with trembling fingers that fumbled with the string, a cup of *tisane* by her side.

" We always give *maman* a *calmant* after her *déjeuner*," explained the wife of the patron, nodding her head towards the little tea-pot.

I wondered what there could possibly be to excite the poor old lady, sitting in that great empty shop waiting for customers that seldom came ; a stimulant would, it seemed to me, be more appropriate.

The outside porter of a flourishing grocery store, a small wrinkled old man, is one of the many friends of Mademoiselle, who, to his great delight, gave him a sprig of mistletoe when he admired the great boss of it she carried.

No, his health had not been very good lately, he confessed in answer to her inquiry ; he had always *mal aux reins*. At the *clinique* the doctors prescribed him rest and sunshine—he threw an ironical glance first at the load of parcels to be delivered and then at the pouring sky, and shrugged his thin shoulders. Then he whispered to Mademoiselle that he was trying to cure himself by wearing a little woollen belt knitted for him when he was a small boy by his *pauvre maman*. She loved her son, and it seemed to him that the love in the belt might help him more than the clever doctors could. " I tell Mademoiselle because she will understand—she will not laugh at me."

Indeed she did not laugh.

We piled our parcels into her Baby Peugeot until its camion-back was nearly broken by the load of toys, turkeys, and bulky goods hastily thrust into bags at the Monoprix, and we drove back into the mountains at about ten miles an hour in that blinding rain.

Arrived at the Château, instead of the eye of a suspicious monk, a welcoming light gleamed through the *grille* in the ancient oak door, and inside the house fires of crackling olive logs burned in the great open fireplaces. We spent a busy evening apportioning presents, packing them up in white paper, tying them with scarlet ribbon, and writing suitable messages ready for delivery the next day—Christmas Eve.

In the morning I drove over to my Domaine near Grasse to take Emilia, who was still caretaking there, her personal present and a turkey almost as big as her small fat self to regale her and her family on Christmas Day.

When she saw it her black eyes rolled heavenward, her pretty little mouth pursed into an ' O ' of astonishment, she clapped both hands upon her thighs and threw her small body backwards in delight. The *beau dinde*, duly pinched, patted, weighed (it was 9 kilos.—18 lb.), and admired from all angles, Madame was enthusiastically embraced whilst being scolded for spending so much money upon Emilia.

The Odyssey of that particular turkey was recounted to me some days later. First it travelled with Emilia in the autocar from Grasse to Villefranche, where lives her widowed sister. Emilia told me that the bus conductor told her that she ought to buy a separate ticket for the turkey as well as her own, for it was nearly as big as she.

The family at Villefranche were obliged to lug the turkey to a baker's shop to be cooked, " for neither threats nor entreaties " would persuade it to enter the home oven. They feasted upon it at noon on Christmas Day, and then Emilia, kissing them all farewell, tucked the mangled monster bird into a basket and travelled back in the great autobus to St François, two or three kilometres beyond Grasse, to the cottage of her married brother, whose family supped upon that turkey till they could feast no more. What remained of it was packed into a parcel and carried back to Grasse to cheer the loneliness of Emilia's widower brother-in-law. His cat finished the last bone.

That turkey, whole and in parts, travelled 120 kilometres and fed more people than its own weight in pounds, a triumphant end to the life of any bird.

When Emilia became a little calmer, together we packed the pheasants she had cooked for the masons and their dessert and tobacco into large baskets, and loaded them, and ourselves, into the car. I felt that the cook must certainly share the fun of preparing the feast for the men and receive their compliments upon her cooking.

Back again at the Château, I found the Baby Peugeot standing in the courtyard. Mademoiselle had just come home after delivering her load of turkeys and toys, much touched and embarrassed by the tears and blessings they had evoked in all the humble homes she had visited.

I begged her to come with Emilia and me to help prepare our ' surprise ' for the masons while they were still at work, and together we climbed the mountain to my small property, laughing at little bright-eyed, puffing Emilia, who wasted all her breath in chatter.

We arranged planks on boulders in the old kitchen around a large slab of wood to serve as table, and set out our feast in readiness. Mademoiselle stuck sprigs of holly and mistletoe in jam-pots, and we laid crackers among the plates.

The masons had improvised a cooking apparatus for themselves, an old stove discarded by the Italian peasants, which Dante had placed in the centre of the room with a pipe attached to it, which was pushed out of a gaping window.

Emilia lit a fire to heat up her pheasants, and between us we roughly boarded up the void doors of the room to keep out the very cold wind that was whistling through the house.

Then we called the men and having shaken hands all round and wished them a happy Christmas, we departed, leaving them to feast together at their ease.

As I was walking through the olive grove on the way to the Château I was shyly hailed by Dante, who had followed me out of the cottage. He tiptoed towards me beaming all over his face, and holding in both hands a lovely bouquet of pink carnations and asparagus fern, a gift from himself and his wife.

Thinking of the precious francs that had been spared from the family stocking—or mattress—to buy those flowers ; remembering that in the spring Dante and his wife were expecting their first baby, and that every *sou* was being saved for the hoped-for son and heir, I could find no words that adequately expressed what I was feeling, but I hope he saw it in my eyes as I stammered out my thanks: "*Ces belles fleurs—magnifiques—tellement touchée—milles remerciments*," and so on, and we somehow got away from each other very conscious of our legs and arms.

Later we all stole back to the cottage, reaching the top floor by the little private door on the north side which led into what would one day be my writing-room, so that we could hear the sounds of revelry in the kitchen below without making the men self-conscious by our presence.

There was a great cracking noise going on down there to the accompaniment of gusts of laughter.

"They've reached the nut stage," commented Mademoiselle.

Then someone obliged with a very sentimental song, and Emilia, who was listening intently, instantly began to hum the refrain.

"Go down and wish them a happy Christmas, Emilia," I urged her, and, after a certain amount of feigned reluctance, she started clambering down the scaffolding into the kitchen below. Her appearance was greeted by a roar of welcome from the revellers. Of course she knew them all—I have yet to meet an inhabitant of the neighbourhood whom Emilia does not know—and there followed fulsome compliments upon her cooking.

Knowing that she was now in her element, Mademoiselle and I felt that we might safely leave them all to suck oranges and pull crackers and sing themselves hoarse, while we went back to the Château to eat our own belated luncheon and rest awhile.

Emilia would certainly be conveyed back to the Domaine by one, if not more, of the revellers below.

In the dusk we walked up the mountain to the old *bergerie* to take a toy to the shepherd's baby boy. Framed in the open doorway against a background of flickering firelight, a blue shawl over her head and her dark curly-headed boy clinging to her skirts, stood the shepherd's wife looking exactly like a lovely plump Italian Madonna. Her husband would soon be home, she assured us ; she was listening for the sound of the sheep-bells coming down the mountain. We presented our toy and waited with her awhile to give him a Christmas greeting.

Suddenly her eyes lit up and her lips parted into a smile as she held up a silencing finger, and we heard in the distance the hollow musical notes of hundreds of bells like the sound of a mountain torrent bubbling downhill under great rocks.

The liquid notes grew louder, and presently we saw waves of sheep wash over the rim of the mountain and come flowing down towards the *bergerie* in a silver flood.

The shepherd came first, and when he saw us he waved his long crook in greeting and begged us to wait until he had folded his sheep safely for the night, as he would like to show us his lambs. His dog nosed the flock into their pens and the shepherd guided the ewes that were with young into a warm shed. Then, lighting an old horn lantern, he beckoned us to follow him into a dark doorway under the *bergerie*.

We found ourselves in a long low shed built up against the natural rock of the mountain which formed a jutting wall of huge grey boulders roofed in with thatch of broom supported by great boles of trees. The ground was strewn with clean straw amid which gambolled white lambs, black lambs, and the tight-curled black-and-white lambs of Italy, adorable people with cheerful waggling tails. The shepherd caressed their little heads as they frisked up to him and snuffled his trousers, while his wife stood near with her beautiful dark-eyed boy in her arms, smiling happily.

For the first time I could picture the Christmas scene in Bethlehem as it really was, and the simple beauty of it robbed me of speech.

Back at the Château, knowing that they would want to go to Midnight Mass, we told the servants that they might all be free for the night and that we would cook our own supper. They whispered that they had prepared ' a surprise ' for Madame and Mademoiselle in their own little sitting-room opening out of the kitchen, and so we decided to sup there.

First we roasted a partridge on a delightful automatic spit which one winds up with a key, and which then revolves slowly before an open fire, ringing a bell when it needs rewinding. This we did in the great *salon* upstairs, and while our bird twirled gracefully before the crackling olive logs, smelling deliciously, we each secretly filled a Christmas stocking for the other in opposite corners of the room, hanging them inside the huge canopied chimney when they were filled to bursting.

Then we hurried our sizzling partridge downstairs to the little servants' hall.

The ' surprise ' they had prepared for us was a little Christmas tree decorated with oyster shells and snail shells slung on the branches, filled with oil and tiny wicks, and then lit—a lovely form of illumination. They had made stars and hearts and tiny boxes of split palm leaves cleverly twisted and plaited ; and had hung chocolates, wrapped in glittering tinted paper, and gilded walnuts on every branch to give colour and light.

The tree was fixed into a curved wooden platform which was raised about a foot from the ground. Over it and under it thick moss had been strewn so that a green cave was formed under the tree, and this they had transformed into a primitive *crêche* with crudely painted cows and donkeys modelled in plaster, all lying in recumbent positions because the Provençal idea is that the beasts in the stable all lay down so that their breath might warm the Holy Child in His low wooden manger.

This Divine Baby was modelled in wax and tucked cosily inside a chocolate *sabot*, surrounded by the Virgin Mary, St Joseph, and kneeling peasants offering loaves of bread and jars of oil and wine.

It was one of the sweetest, quaintest *crêches* I have ever seen, and when we beheld our ' surprise ' and saw all the minute and patient work that had been put into it, at last we realised why it was that the work of the house had been somewhat neglected for the past fortnight and why no one downstairs had ever answered a bell until it had been rung twice or thrice.

Mademoiselle and I shared our little Christmas feast by the light of the illumined tree, having much difficulty in preventing the greedy Tucker from devouring the baby in that chocolate *sabot* and thus ruining the *crêche*. Then we went upstairs into the *salon* to unpack our stockings.

First we each placed a candle outside on the window-sill and lit them for ' our wishes.' This is another Provençal custom, the idea being that the candle-beam will guide the wish—or prayer—of each person to the right destination. Then we spent a happy half-hour untying our little parcels (even the two dogs had their individual presents) and looking at our Christmas cards. There were the usual conventional robins, snowy churches, holly and mistletoe, and mediæval and Victorian country scenes, from England; modern, very decorative, and bold designs from America; and the gay and glittering French variety, including a lady clad only in a *maillot* with a bouquet of holly pressed against her tumpkin, which ornament looked very prickly and uncomfortable. There were also some very lovely painted *crêches* built in cardboard with effects of lighting gained by cutting away the cardboard and substituting transparent paper of different colours, so that when placed before a candle or electric light the star in the east with its shaft of light pointing to the stable, the stable window with its view of star-spangled sky, the haloes of the Madonna and of the surrounding angels, glow with mysterious light.

When we had arranged our gifts and cards around the room amid the branches of blossoming peach and almond (cut off before the frost so that they might bloom in vases indoors), we turned on the wireless and listened to the Christmas carols in England.

And so to bed.

Next morning, Christmas Day, the rain had ceased ; the sun shone in a marvellously blue sky, and everywhere the wet olive leaves glistened like silver. There was that wonderful smell of spring in the air that stirs the imagination and warms the heart. As I sniffed in the delicious fragrance of it from my bedroom window I heard the excited yells of the village children down below the olive groves. Evidently they had been given their toys and were rejoicing over the gifts of *Père Noël*.

Everywhere church bells chimed and tolled, seemingly without rhyme or reason in their irregular rhythm, but each, as I have now learned, having its own particular message or meaning. For instance, during the month of May (the month of Mary) the great Mary bell in Grasse tolls every day at certain hours, and all the shrines dedicated to the Virgin are lit with candles throughout the month. Mademoiselle has a tiny one in a niche of an old wall hung with ferns, and every night of May in her secret garden one sees the glimmer of the little oil *veilleuse* lamp glowing in the darkness and the pale Madonna behind it in her fern grotto guarding the Château.

A procession of peasants and children trailed up to the house this Christmas morning to *toucher la main de Mademoiselle,* thank her for her presents, and wish her joy. I saw the wife of my gardener coming up the drive with her small sister, both laden with enormous bouquets of flowers. One, of carnations, roses, and mimosa, from herself and Antonio her husband, was presented to me, and one to Mademoiselle; and yet another from Mademoiselle's gardener (father of mine) for Mademoiselle, and one for me. The whole *salon* was filled with flowers before the morning passed.

One thundering knock upon the front door announced a young gentleman of about twelve years old dressed, as I imagined from their dimensions and eccentric fit, in his father's trousers and cap. Neither Mademoiselle nor I had ever seen him before. When she asked him why he had come and whence, he grinned up at her in a delightfully friendly way, pointed to the mountain above, and told us that he had said to himself, " *Tu vas dire le bon jour à ces dames en bas.*"

The Christmas spirit. He had trudged five miles down an appalling mountain track just to greet two strange ladies on Christmas Day.

Of course he got a franc from us each and some oranges and nuts, but I honestly do not believe that he came to the Château in hope, because the moment he had blurted out his little greeting he pulled off his ridiculous cap, made us a bow, and turned abruptly on his heel to depart. The next arrival was a miniature woman with high heels, the fashionable *béret* perched over one bistred eye, plucked eyebrows, and a small made-up *à la mode* face. She proved to be the sixteen-year-old daughter of the village postmistress, the eldest of a family of six, who through precocity and intelligence had been early placed as telephonist in the *Grand Bureau des Postes* of a large neighbouring town. She had come home for her Christmas holiday and was helping *maman* in the tiny village post office, a great boon for us because, since she came back, we had been able to understand our telegrams. Before then they were very amusing but quite unintelligible. I received the following :—

MADAME LADY CHATU FORTEQ.<br>KOG STADY LUW BITI.

which, being interpreted, was " Château Fortescue. Coming Saturday. Love. Betty." A telephoned telegram.

The little lady, who temporarily transmitted local telegrams accurately, brought us each a knitted scarf made by *maman*. How ? And when ? we wondered. *Maman* dresses, cooks for, and manages her young and unruly tribe of five, cleans her house, and tends her garden, rabbits, and chickens in the intervals of selling stamps, depositing the savings of the village, taking telephone messages, and despatching telegrams. Where she found the *sous* to buy the wool for those scarves and the time to knit them for us remains a touching mystery.

To send a telephone message from her office is an agony both for her and for oneself. The poor patient little woman winds the handle of her obsolete machine to call the Exchange, wails " 'Ullo ! Grasse ! 'Ullo ! GRASSE ! 'ULLO ! GRASSE ! " at intervals in a despairing voice, holding the receiver close to her weary head with one hand, while with the other she signals frantic and peremptory inhibitions to her children, who, seeing *maman* chained safely to the apparatus, are invariably doing something forbidden with an unholy glee.

After a while she gives up in despair, leans against the counter, and tells one a little bit of pathetic family history : *petit Paul* has croup ; *Henri* wears out his boots terribly fast ; one of her handsomest rabbits died mysteriously in the night. Each child in turn is dragged from the poky living-room under the darned dividing curtain into the post office to be presented to Madame, and although they drive *maman* nearly crazy, one knows that she adores all her children and is very proud of them.

After a time the little woman winds the handle of her telephone again and wails, " *'Ullo! Grasse!* " patiently once more.

" *Tst—Tst—Châteauneuf au milieu—Ah!* " she sighs, as a subscriber from a neighbouring village crosses the line just as she has succeeded in attracting the attention of supercilious Grasse.

In mercy I tell her that my message is not important and leave her beaming gratitude, patient, plucky little woman, and she rushes into her kitchen to stir her vegetable soup.

The Christmas visitors all duly greeted, thanked, and despatched, I leaped into my car and drove to the Grand Hotel in Grasse for my Christmas service. English residents and visitors were then so scarce that we could not afford to open the English Church, which is entirely supported by voluntary contributions ; the expenses and stipend of the Chaplain (which he seldom sees as he nobly pays the other church expenses first), the organist's fees, the cost of altar flowers, the cleaning and heating — all very costly with the franc at 74 to the £ as it was then. A large room in the Grand Hotel has now been transformed into a temporary chapel, and very lovely it has been made. Here the Chaplain holds services during the season, and here I had my Christmas celebration amid a handful of English, very thankful to get a Christmas service at all.

On the way back to the Château I met old Hilaire, our gardener during " Monsieur's " lifetime. He spied me from afar and began a kind of grotesque dance on the footpath, baring his old bald head and waving his cap in a frenzy to attract my attention, which never could have missed that familiar face and form.

" *Bon jour, Madame ! Comment ça va ? Bien, j'espère, toujours bien ? J'ai languissé voir Madame et de toucher sa main.*"

We shook hands long and with violence. He had lost more front teeth, poor old Hilaire, and he looked much thinner. Years of hard manual labour have tired his gallant heart and he had a *crise cardiaque* this summer, he told me, and had to be carried home, but was working again now. I sympathised with him and he cheered up and began to joke in his old Rabelaisian manner. Referring to the recent sharp frost and bitterly cold weather, he said it had been " *Un temps pour les amoureux.*" Knowing my Hilaire, I did not ask him to explain. Then he launched upon reminiscences of " *le pauvre Monsieur bien-aimé* " until the past nearly overwhelmed me with its

179

flood of precious memories, and I excused myself, bade old Hilaire farewell, and drove on.

Mademoiselle and I ate our Christmas turkey accompanied by fresh Brussels sprouts cooked with whole Spanish chestnuts, and tender lettuces from the Château garden. For dessert we ate our own oranges, kakis, and physalis (Cape gooseberries), and then we went upstairs to smoke our cigarettes in the *salon* and wait for King George V., of beloved memory, to talk to us.

It was so wonderful to hear that well-known voice greeting ' his family ' scattered about the world in all his vast Empire ; so miraculous to hear him speaking to us clearly across sea and mountains, woods and plains. He would have been touched, I think, had he known of the love and loyalty shown him by the English in Provence, or could have seen them rush to the wireless to hear his heartening voice giving them its last fatherly message.

I had often wished that he could hear of the party given on his birthday by one of the oldest residents out here, a very great lady, deservedly beloved, to which every English man and woman, rich or poor, in the district had been invited to share in the celebration. How, when her friends had served themselves and each other to a cold supper in order that the English servants chauffeurs, and gardeners should feast undisturbed at the same time, everyone was called into her *salon* to drink the health of the King, proposed by an old General, and drunk even by our hostess's great-great-niece, who was brought down, blinking drowsily, in her pink blanket by her Nanny and propped upright upon the dining-room table.

One of the company, a fine old gardener who once worked at Kew, was led around the room by his hostess and introduced to us all as a Personage. He became so patriotic and exhilarated by champagne that he ended by wishing *me* many happy returns of the day and a long and prosperous reign.

I drove back to the Domaine in the starlight. The night was so warm and the air so full of heavenly scents and night sounds that I stopped the car under a great wall of grey rocks studded with green glow-worms and drank in the fragrance and peace of it as I watched the fireflies flickering among the pine trees, and the silver sickle of the moon sink below the rim of the mountains until only one radiant blade pointed in the sky.

I thought of all I loved in England, of the King who, because of his life of service for his Empire, could never know this peace. I heard the voice of "Monsieur" say: "The King is the hardest-worked man in his Dominions." I remembered those days at Windsor, during the war, when a continuous stream of telegraph boys flowed to the Castle bringing the King despatches from the Front, and messages from all over the world, so that even at dinner he was obliged to keep a pad of telegraph forms by his side in order that he might write immediate replies. How, when he had dismissed his Household for the night at 10 P.M., he went into his study with his private secretary and started work again. . . . Thinking of these things, I hoped that as the moon sank behind the mountains on his birthday night, our King, too, might have sunk into sleep.

And now, as Mademoiselle and I listened to his Christmas message, never dreaming that it was his last, I thought that the vibrant voice sounded a little tired—as well it might.

Well, he has gained that well-earned peace at last. God rest him now. . . .

# CHAPTER X.

## BENEDICTION.

In January, Dante, whose smiling chubby face had heartened me throughout delays and deluges, suddenly lost his mother. The poor old woman, who had been paralysed for many years and had lost her wits so that she could not even recognise her son, died suddenly one morning whilst he was at work, and the activities of Dante became paralysed too.

He could not forgive his relations for not having sent for him at once, even if he could do nothing. He could not forget that when he had returned home for his *déjeuner* he had found that his mother had been dead for some hours. Even the neighbours had known of her decease before her own son, and that, apparently, he could not bear.

For days we saw him no more, and, of course, the work suffered, for the two remaining masons and their assistants were without initiative, and once again my architect was stricken down with influenza.

I did the best I could, trying to keep the men busy with fool-proof jobs and working myself in my garden, planting belated bulbs and iris in the rock-garden and under the olive trees so that I could supervise building operations. But there were hours when I had to be at the Château to tend my invalid, and, during my absences, I found that the work did not progress very quickly.

I had great hopes that I could put the men on to the arranging of the cave which was to contain my central heating plant and supply of coke or coal, because, if their work there proved inartistic, only the gardener who stoked the stove would remark it. But once again the pigeons baulked me. They had made a nest in the rafters and could not be disturbed.

Already we had been delayed by rains, by the Festivals of All Souls and All Saints, Christmas and the New Year. Soon February and the Bishop would be upon us. I had as yet received no word of an altar and benches for my chapel ; and I was becoming terribly discouraged.

Then at last came the joyful news that a Louis XIII. altar and six rough wooden benches had been discovered for me in Aix-en-Provence. *La Chapelle des Pénitents Bleus* had been destroyed many years ago and a pious man had saved the altar, fearing that a secular-minded person might purchase it and use it as a sideboard. He had stored it safely away, with the benches, in his loft, hoping that some day they might again be honoured in a consecrated place. He was willing to let me have them for my chapel at a ridiculously low price if I would pay for their transport.

What incredible luck ! Even a searing mistral, bruising my shrubs and early stocks, and blowing sand and *débris* through my doorless cottage ; even the mournful face of Dante who appeared that morning heavily banded with crape, and with a mouth forming an inverted ' U ' instead of an ' O,' could not depress me very much.

I raced in to Mademoiselle with my news, knowing that it would cheer her tardy con-valescence, and she was as delighted as I.

" They are extraordinarily clever and energetic, those two," she said, referring to our Frenchman and his Russian lady partner. " They always find exactly what one wants in the end, even if they have to scour the whole of Provence to do it."

The altar arrived some days later : a very lovely thing in faintly gilded wood with the arms of some Cardinal or Archbishop carved boldly upon it. The gilding was so worn and rubbed that the natural wood beneath was apparent, and because of this dim, ancient look, when posed in the recess under the great arch, it looked wonderful.

A beautiful wooden cross, rescued from the same chapel, had been sent with it, and this I fixed to a post and placed a few inches behind and above the altar. Then I fetched the masons to lug in the smaller of the two circular stone troughs that we had discovered in the caves, and this we posed upon a great chunk of rock near the door to form a primitive font. The benches had not yet arrived, but already my chapel was transformed.

I remembered a wrought-iron gate discarded from the Domaine long since which would form an entrance to the little cloister where once had lived the rabbits, and this was sent for and fixed into the outer wall. The chapel now only lacked a door. Where could I find one old and massive enough ?

" Send an S.O.S. to St Tropez : that couple will find you as many ancient doors as you want. They always achieve the impossible," said Mademoiselle.

And she was right, as usual, for in a week or two they had discovered doors enough to shut in house and chapel ; the loveliest old doors of walnut and of oak, taken from a derelict *château* of very early date ; massive panelled doors of dark well-seasoned wood, from which, mercifully, their lovely locks, hinges, and decorative iron-work had not been removed. These arrived with the benches for the chapel, the quaintest little benches with wooden kneelers attached to them, and so arranged that while kneeling one was well supported by the seat. Dear little benches. Comfy little benches.

Mademoiselle had by this time recovered enough to go out for short feeble walks in the January sunshine, and I longed for the moment when her wobbly legs would be strong enough to climb up to the cottage ; for there was much to show and to ask her.

" Dante's face is enough to give one a relapse," she remarked when at last that joyful day came. " Is he still mourning that mother ? And does he have to cease work during this prolonged period of mourning, for I notice that he, personally, is doing nothing."

It was too true. Since the donning of those crape bands Dante had mooned about the place giving instructions to the other masons in a sepulchral tone, but doing nothing beside save advertise his bereavement.

However, at the reappearance of his architect, I noticed that the crape-banded coat was swiftly removed and a trowel taken up by a hitherto nerveless hand. He had known Mademoiselle for many years, and perhaps realised that she had little sympathy for those who allowed personal

187

grief to interfere with their duties. Before she left he had actually contrived to smile.

She was thrilled with the chapel, and forthwith hung a beautiful bronze Christ, which she had found buried in Flanders mud during the war, above the stone font. We then placed the two tall iron candle-sticks with their gigantic cathedral candles, which Mademoiselle had given me for Christmas, one each side of the altar, and an old rustic plaster figure of the Virgin and Child in the window leading into the cloister, so that from inside the chapel She was seen framed by the green garden beyond, and from outside the peasants, if they hesitated to enter a Protestant chapel, could open the iron gate and place their flowers at Her feet. I wanted everyone to feel that they could come there.

The chapel was now finished and ready for the Bishop. The cottage had walls, ceilings, doors, but no windows or staircase, the old one, alas! having collapsed. To reach the upper floor the Bishop would have to clamber up scaffolding. Could he ? Would he ?

Mademoiselle had promised to support me during the little ceremony when he came, but the day of his coming (my birthday, marked by a gay picture post-card from Emilia depicting a golden horse-shoe garlanded with roses, lilies, and forget-

me-nots) dawned grey and cheerless, mist shrouded
the mountains, a fine rain fell at intervals, and
everything outside was sopping wet. It would
have been madness for one so recently convalescent
to stand about in that damp atmosphere, and I
realised that I must be the only congregation
during that little service. " When two or three
are gathered together . . .," I quoted softly to
myself. Well, anyway, there would be two.

I had told the masons to take a day off, so that
we had the place to ourselves, and when I mounted
early to the cottage I found it swept and garnished
and the usual array of workmen's coats, slippers,
and tools hidden away somewhere.

I cut off great branches of almond blossom to
decorate my chapel, laid the fair linen upon the
altar, and lit my candles. The Bishop had promised
to bring with him all things necessary for the
celebration of Holy Communion. Then I went
back to the Château to await his arrival.

At half-past eleven a car drove into the courtyard and a tall thin Bishop, whose build and old-
world courtesy of manner reminded me instantly
of " Monsieur," alighted from it.

Together we climbed the terraces to the cottage,
and I took him first into the chapel. I think the
curious mixture within may have puzzled him a
little : the altar bearing the arms of some prince

of the Roman Church ; the figure of the Madonna and Child dominating the little cloister with massed flowers at Her feet, together with the symbols of the Anglican Church. But he said nothing, and I loved him for his silence. After all, we are all striving to reach the same goal by different paths.

He asked me to leave him alone for a few minutes while he made his preparations, and I returned to find him standing before the altar, framed by that wonderful arch, the candle-light sparkling upon his golden vestments and the tip of his mitre nearly touching the vaulted ceiling. A picture I can never forget.

I took my place upon one of those small rough benches, and that most moving and comforting of all services began.

When it was over, the Bishop dedicated the chapel to the memory of my Beloveds, and then, staff in hand, he preceded me up the stone stairway and into the cottage. There he gave me a little pamphlet containing the service used when blessing a house and asked me to say the responses. . . .

Where—oh, WHERE had I left my spectacles ? For I have just reached the age when my arms are not long enough to read small print. I realised that those spectacles were far beyond

reach down at the Château and that my only hope
lay in my memory. Perhaps when I heard the
familiar sentences my early up-bringing in clerical
circles would help me to remember the responses.
But—would the sentences be familiar ? I could
not explain my predicament to the Bishop who
had already begun the little service, and I experienced the same feeling of panic that I had
felt as a very small girl clad in a stiff pink pinafore
finding herself to be the only congregation at
matins in a small country church, seated in a tall
oak pew and obliged to read alternate verses of
the psalm of the day with a surpliced father. I
remembered how, inevitably, I had, as I dreaded
I should, come upon a terribly long and unpronounceable word, had faltered and paused, then
cast beseeching eyes towards that dear figure, and
the surge of relief as I saw the twinkle in his and
heard a gentle voice prompting me encouragingly.

If I faltered now, would the Bishop twinkle and
then prompt ? I feared not. Mercifully the
sentences were familiar, and I was able to respond
as we passed from room to room on the ground
floor and each in turn were blest.

There remained the top floor, but no staircase
to reach it. The Bishop paused for a second
below the scaffolding planks and I wondered if
he would tell me that, robed as he was with staff

and book in hand, he could not attempt the ascent. But no, he gallantly gathered his golden vestments around him and somehow managed the precarious climb, I scrambling after him.

The little indoor ceremony over, we went out into the garden. Undeterred by the fine soft rain—which I feared would ruin those wonderful robes, yet knew that I could not offer to hold an umbrella over them—the Bishop walked through it blessing my vines, my olive trees, and my little jessamine terraces that they might bear abundance of fruit and flowers. He even walked up to the site of what will one day be my garage, if times improve, and striding over *débris*, clambering over piles of sand and stones, he blest my future goings-out and comings-in, a glorious figure against a background of misty mountains and grey olive trees.

Suddenly I saw the scared face of a peasant peering over a neighbouring wall. He clapped his hand over his mouth, evidently to hold in a shout of excitement, and then the head vanished to reappear a few moments later flanked by others with equally round eyes and mouths. The Bishop finished blessing the heaps of stones and piles of sand, quite unaware of his congregation of awed peasants ; and then, the little ceremony over, he walked back to the chapel there to take off his vestments.

I waited for him, sitting upon a great boulder under the olive trees, praying funny little lonely prayers. " Try not to be stiff or formal or over-orthodox with God," a beloved bishop in England once wrote to me. " Take God, as it were, into your confidence. I think He wants us to be more at our ease with Him and to tell Him frankly what we really think."

Well, I did that now, perched upon my rock, thinking of the new life I must soon begin to live alone in the cottage ; and, during that little conversation, I quoted the Hind in " Monsieur's " ' The Story of a Red Deer,' asking that whatever happened to me I might " never, never, never lie down and squeal " ; that I might always preserve a sense of proportion and a sense of humour ; that I might always be NECESSARY to someone, and lots of little things like that. Above all, I prayed that in this small house I might find peace.

It was then that a shaft of sunlight pierced through the mist pointing to the chapel, and suddenly from out its door flew a bird.

Not the dove of peace, only one of my pigeons, but it seemed to me like a symbol. . . . And then I smiled as I thought that, after all, *three* had been gathered together for that little service, the Bishop, my pigeon, and I—three, and an invisible Fourth.

## CHAPTER XI.

### GOOD-BYE, GALLANT COMPANY.

"WITH one stride came the Spring," to misquote Coleridge. Suddenly my olive grove was starred with scarlet anemones and tiny wild tulips; the aubretia cuttings taken from the Domaine and pushed in between great rocks had formed flat cushions of verdure, and were now splashed with every shade of mauve and purple; sprays of tender peach-blossom flushed against a sky of vivid blue; wild violets carpeted the rock-garden, and the terrace below became one solid sheet of blue as the Russian violets burst simultaneously into bloom.

Down in the Château garden a golden mimosa shimmered in the sunshine, reflected in the turquoise water of the great swimming-pool, which Guiseppe, Mademoiselle's old Italian gardener, had emptied and sprayed with sulphate of copper during the autumn to kill all weeds and moss. Arum lilies and purple Provençal iris peered over its brink to look at their lovely forms pictured in the clear blue water. There were even a few early pink roses clustering upon the old grey walls.

In England Spring comes so shyly, heralded by a few tiny aconites and snowdrops who, doubtless, realise that they will very likely have their noses bitten by frost for daring to appear so early. Then all the lovely delicate flowers, wild violets, primroses, daffodils, crocuses, and catkins take courage and blossom in their turn until, sure of a welcoming sun, cowslips and cuckoo flowers spangle the meadows, kingcups fringe the little streams, and woodland glades are ablaze with bluebells.

Even as I write about the slow and rapturous awakening of Spring in England after the long and cruel winter, I can recapture the thrill I always had on finding the first white violets under a fairy silver birch in our garden at home, and knew that Spring was hiding somewhere in the woods and would soon appear.

In Provence Spring comes so suddenly that I always feel as if Nature had gathered all her flowers at once, had massed them into one great bouquet and presented it to me one lovely morning. But out here during the winter there are always flowers of some sort, and the sun never leaves us desolate and dreary for very long, so that the joy of Spring in Provence is perhaps less than in England. To joy intensely one must have suffered first.

Still, as I climbed the mountain towards my cottage I experienced that delicious gaiety of spirit that only Spring can give. Birds were making love in the trees ; old Guiseppe reported that all the rabbits were with young ; the pigeons were sitting tight upon eggs ; and the electrician and plumber were hard at work giving light and water to my new home. Everything was burgeoning and spouting and flashing in the hot sunshine.

When it was first rumoured that I had bought and was about to arrange a cottage a few kilometres away from our Domaine, all the Grasse workmen who had enlarged and beautified it for us had come to ask me to employ them once more. They were old friends and they knew that "Monsieur" and I had been delighted with their work. But I had decided early that it would be only fair to employ the local tradesmen who were all waiting with expectant eyes hoping for orders. This I explained to my friends, who were sorrowfully obliged to agree that my decision was just.

But, happily for me, there was no plumber in the village where I was taking up my residence, and so of course I engaged my old Grasse friend to do the work for me, the most excellent plumber in Provence.

His *chef plombier* arrived, quiet but proud, holding out the little finger of his right hand for me to grasp in greeting. I remembered that "Monsieur" had remarked: "Dammit, the man greeted me in the manner of the old Duke," and then told me that the Duke of Wellington offered only his little finger to his friends. Perhaps it was condescension in the Duke's case. In that of the *chef* it was consideration, for his hands were generally wet or sticky.

Thenceforth he adopted me as his especial care, saving me every possible evitable expense. I wanted millions of taps in my garden to facilitate watering in summer, and I was informed that each tap cost twenty francs, and that, to begin with, I could perfectly manage with but three. Joints would be left where extra taps could be added when times improved in France. The *chef* was for ever thinking of devices whereby he could adapt fittings for my comfort, cutting a double-railed nickel pipe for drying towels in half so that it would serve two bathrooms, and so on ; even making me two rough cylindrical altar-vases from a piece of lead piping when I confided to him that nothing I could buy for my chapel would ever look primitive enough for that ancient setting.

He also invented a cunning and delightful system of pierced piping whereby I could spray the flat roof-terrace above my bedroom (planned by Mademoiselle to facilitate sun-bathing and provide a wondrous panoramic view) to keep it —and myself—cool in summer. All I should have to do when hot or annoyed was to climb a small stairway leading to my roof-terrace and turn on my cold douche.

There was no end to the ingenuity of the *chef plombier*. I fell into the old habit of yelling for him whenever I or one of the workmen were in any difficulty whatsoever, and always he solved our problems in his calm paternal manner. He worked with all his usual quiet energy, silent and unsmiling as of yore, though his face did once relax when I inquired after *le fils héritier ;* for a son and heir had been born to him whilst working for us at the Domaine, and " Monsieur," in perfect but archaic French, had next day congratulated him upon the arrival of *un fils héritier*.

Everyone made use of the *chef ;* even Asunta's temporary substitutes at the Château rushed up the hill to find him when they had forgotten to order meat for the household, and the *chef* brought back a red beef-steak swinging from the handles of his bicycle when he returned from Grasse after his *déjeuner*. Nothing could upset his Olympian calm or thwart his utter efficiency.

And then one day I met another old friend. The

beautiful giant carpenter who had also worked for us at the Domaine, and who, on the day of the *cabade*, when the workmen had celebrated the completion of the roof in Provençal fashion and we had given them a feast, had honoured me with a respectful kiss upon the brow, to my intense embarrassment and " Monsieur's " great amusement and delight.

My giant Pierre now appeared to solicit orders for the cottage. He had married a wife.

" She is tiny, I expect ? " I asked at once. Yes, she only reached his elbow, Pierre informed me, grinning shyly. Huge men nearly always marry tiny women, and are thereafter bullied by them.

He had now set up for himself as an *artisan*, employing one workman. He had put all his savings into his little *commerce*, and was naturally anxious to secure a *clientèle*.

" Madame was always satisfied with my work at the Domaine," he pleaded in his bubbling bass voice. " I made those bookcases after the design of " Monsieur " for his many books. I should like Madame to have a souvenir of Pierre in her new home."

All very touching and insidious ; but remembering that I had promised to employ only local tradesmen, and had already given orders for my window-frames to a dear carpenter in the village, I strove to harden my heart and to explain the situation to Pierre.

Yes, he had already been informed of the decision of Madame, and had gone that morning to visit the local carpenter, who had assured him that it would be impossible to finish the work of Madame without outside help, and had been very glad to know that the services of Pierre were available. Far be it from Madame to upset so amicable an arrangement which was also so pleasing to herself. I beamed upon Pierre, and we shook hands happily over this comfortable combination.

Thenceforth I was to see Pierre riding up to my cottage upon an antediluvian bicycle, miraculously balancing himself with a door under each arm, a few planks on his shoulders, and often something upon his head, for he wished to save Madame the expense of their transport by lorry. How he could manage to ride all the way from Grasse, thus loaded, upon that ancient solid-tyred bicycle remains to me a mystery.

Always Pierre brought me messages from Emilia. They had been at school together, she in the senior class when he was among the babies ; but they had remained great friends, and although herself only reaching to his waist-line, she still preserved the maternal protective manner she had then adopted towards the infant Pierre. I knew that Emilia had prompted him *aller un peu voir Madame*, knowing of his recent marriage, his need of work, and, doubtless, of my weakness for *le géant*, as "Monsieur" and I had always called him.

Pierre assured me that Emilia was sick of caretaking at the Domaine. "*Elle languisse pour Madame*," he said. When did Madame think of arranging her *déménagement* from the Domaine ?

I remembered that Emilia adores household removals, whereas even the prospect of one makes me feel weak in the head and knees, and her reminder of what lay ahead of us decided me to fix the grisly date.

For weeks I had been making lists of the furniture I should need in the cottage, and plans of the rooms with copious notes as to where each object taken from the Domaine should be placed. The great bookshelves had already been removed and adapted to line the walls of my writing-room, and Monsieur's books (save seventy old and rare volumes on matters military which had been sent to Aldershot ; and the first copy published of each of his works which had always been given to me with a precious inscription and which accompanied me everywhere) were packed with my poets and classics, and had long awaited rearrangement. But I had a new idea for lighting my studio invisibly. Its walls were painted a soft pale grey; the floor was tiled with grey square tiles; the doors and bookcases painted dead white with a new form of dull washable paint; scarlet curtains and carpet were already ordered, and I intended to arrange my deep-blue Bristol glass along the top of the bookcases (which reach only half-way up the walls) and illumine it at night with hidden daylight electric lamps. My clever Russian electrician had also hidden lamps in the door and window recesses to illumine the scarlet curtains, and when my white chair covers arrived I was very hopeful of a daring but rather lovely room.

But the planning and installation of that lighting had taken time, and success was only obtained after several bad failures. It is not always easy to gain the effect of which one has dreamed, and in the meanwhile those hundreds of books had languished in their packing-cases.

Another agony had been the pictures with which the Domaine was lined. I brought over our water-colours, which, though they had looked lovely in my pale blue and silver *salon* at the Domaine, looked perfectly poisonous on the walls of my ancient cottage, and were at once pettishly pulled down and taken back to the Domaine.

Then there was "Monsieur's" "Gallant Company," his fifty mezzotints and engravings of famous soldiers of every period which lined his great *Galerie*. Always we had taken our bodyguard with us wherever we went, and now—my cottage was too small to house more than a very few. Which of "Monsieur's" heroes should I take? Oh, WHICH?

And then I had decided that they could not be parted. They had always been together. I would present them, with a portrait of "Monsieur," to the Staff College at Camberley, and the Gallant Company should travel back to England with the Historian of the British Army, who had so proudly chronicled their great deeds. This should be my memorial to him, and I should know his precious collection of soldier portraits safe for all time.

When we first came to live in Provence I had hung them myself in his great *Galerie* at the Domaine in groups which he arranged for me, each in their correct period : Marlborough with his bewigged Generals ; the Peninsular men ; the Indian section, and so on ; and now it was my sad task to take them down from its walls. Each was a familiar friend, and as I laid them one after another upon the floor I seemed to hear again the voice of "Monsieur" telling me anecdotes about each and all as he visited them in turn, eyeglass in eye, every evening of his life.

" Dear old Granby, with his bald head. You know why he is always depicted thus, Sweetheart ? The battle was going against him when his wig blew off, and his discouraged men rallied round that bald head, conspicuous in the sunshine.

" Extraordinary face, Wolfe's : profile like the flap of an envelope, that peak of a nose and the forehead and chin sloping sharply back. But what an able chap."

Then, smiling lovingly at Sir John Moore : " Even the last anguish he endured had not power to contort that beautiful face. He gave no sign of pain, but bore it all with gentleness and patience, his only anxiety being for the welfare of his men."

" I think Sir John Moore is your favourite hero," I once remarked to him, and he replied—

" Yes. I think he is the finest example of a good soldier and a great gentleman that I know."

As I tenderly stacked those portraits ready for their voyage and said good-bye to ' our body-guard,' it comforted me to think that future generations of the soldiers he so loved might find inspiration and courage as they looked upon them —and perhaps think sometimes of the man who spent his life so selflessly in the defence and justification of the British Army.

# CHAPTER XII.

## PERSPIRATION IN PROVENCE.

I was glad when the task of depleting " Monsieur's "
*Galerie* at the Domaine was over, for that hurt the
most. His huge writing-desk was already placed
in my studio in the cottage for my own use : I
knew he would like that. What matter if it
dwarfed the room somewhat, or that its lines are
more massive than elegant ? Its size and its
capacious drawers and cupboards were always
such a joy to him and would still be to me. I had
had his especial possessions taken early to the
cottage by a professional household remover. The
rest of the furniture that I intended to take could
be brought over by a local lorry owned by one
Périgord, a vendor of wood and manure. My
young gardener had the assurance of Monsieur
Périgord that he would take every care of my
things and would bring plenty of straw and
packing-cases to ensure that the furniture was
not scratched.

Accordingly, I hired the lorry of this unknown

gentleman for a certain morning and arranged with Emilia that I should go over to the Domaine with my gardener and dear Russian electrician, who was also a friend of all the little English colony in the village and could always be counted upon to give help in any predicament or emergency. We four could do a great amount of preliminary packing and lug the furniture that I needed out into the now empty garage ready to be transported the next day by Monsieur Périgord. In this way there would be far less risk to the furniture and also to the floors of the Domaine.

When we arrived in *Desirée*, my Fiat car, we found Emilia dancing about on the doorstep, itching to begin dragging furniture about. She had already packed most of the china and glass into huge straw-lined baskets, and the moment I appeared she bombarded me with a fusilade of questions.

Could she take her meat-chopper with her? Surely if Madame let or sold the Domaine she would not leave that *si beau* meat-chopper?

And the *glacière*? And the ironing-board? And, above all, all the jams and preserves that Emilia had made from the produce of the Domaine?

And what about the two stray cats which Emilia had selected as her favourites from the eight who frequented the garden, and which had now become so tame that they even entered the house ?  Cats were always useful things in the home.  They devoured rats and mice and saved Antonio the trouble of emptying the rubbish-pail. If she left the lid off, the pail was always empty in the morning.  Was there already a cat in the cottage ?

There had been a cat, I reflected, but, fortunately, it had been removed with the rest of the menagerie when the Italian family at last departed.  For the hundredth time I had to tell Emilia that I preferred birds to cats, and, there being so few birds left in Provence owing to the sporting tendencies of the Provençaux, I could not bear to see any more massacred by cats.  Also the Château dogs would make their life a hell.  She must find homes for those she had adopted.

But of course we would take with us the handsome meat-chopper and the *glacière* and ironing-board, and most certainly the contents of Emilia's store-cupboard.

We all worked so hard that in a few hours we had accomplished all that was then possible. The fragile things had been packed very carefully, and I decided to take these myself in the back of the car.  The linen and blankets were bestowed in baskets, and all the furniture had been dragged out-of-doors and stacked into the

garage ready for Monsieur Périgord next day.
We had really done the heaviest part of the work
for him, and all he had now to do was to load up
the things into his lorry and to transport them.
I did not see that it was in any way necessary for
me to supervise this loading ; Emilia would be
there, and we had already made his task quite
fool-proof.  Or so I thought then.

All visits to the Domaine were painful to me,
and these last had been worst of all.  Wrenching
out one's roots from familiar soil must always
hurt—and why prolong the agony ?  And so I
told Emilia that I should not accompany Monsieur
Périgord to the Domaine in the heat of the next
morning.  I had engaged him for the whole day,
and he could bring over the things gradually in
several loads and so risk no breakages.  At ten
o'clock I would be waiting at the cottage with
a band of assistants to help him unload the lorry.

Punctually at ten o'clock the next day I went
up to the new home with Mademoiselle, my electrician, and Pierre, the giant carpenter, whose
mighty arms would, I knew, be invaluable ; and
there would be the masons also to help us.

Monsieur Périgord, and a peasant who worked
for him, had left the village at seven o'clock that
morning *en route* for the Domaine accompanied
by my gardener as guide and helper, so that I

expected their arrival with the first load at any moment. But many moments passed and still they did not come. An hour dragged by; two hours—and my assistants all, save Mademoiselle and I, who never care when we eat, began to fidget because the village clock had tolled the hour of noon when all good Provençaux expect to have four feet in the trough. I pleaded for their patience. Monsieur Périgord would surely soon appear with his lorry, and if they deserted me for their *déjeuner* how could two feeble women help to unload heavy furniture ?

Their chivalry aroused, they nobly stifled the call of the stomach, though one of them slyly remarked that perhaps Monsieur Périgord and my gardener were eating their luncheons together somewhere, and that the sating of their appetites was causing this delay. Horrible thought.

At half-past twelve I dismissed my men, not having the heart to keep them any longer, and Mademoiselle and I decided to rush down to the Château, gobble some refreshment, and then quickly return to the cottage to await events.

We awaited those events for three more hours, and I cursed the fact that my telephone had not yet been installed so that I could ring up Emilia and ask her what in the world had happened, and been happening since ten o'clock that morning.

At length, seeing that I was becoming frantic, my electrician volunteered to walk some kilometres to the nearest telephone and make inquiries.

He returned after a long time to tell me that the voice of Emilia had assured him cheerfully that *ces messieurs* were already on their way.

ALREADY on their way? I should hope they were! I longed to hold sweet converse with ' those gentlemen ' when they DID arrive.

Mademoiselle had long since drifted back to the Château, having wasted half a day inside and outside my cottage. My electrician and carpenter had ceased to be facetious (that's a delicious word, containing all the vowels in their right sequence) and were plunged in gloom, and I had left them to perch myself upon the half-built wall of the courtyard, from which vantage-point I could command a view of the little tributary road which flows out of the main traffic-stream to Nice through quiet olive groves towards my front door.

Suddenly my eyes, wearied from watching for that tarrying lorry, espied a huge swaying bulk on the distant *Route Nationale*. Idly I wondered what it might be. Some travelling circus perhaps—a merry-go-round, maybe—when I was electrified by the voice of my electrician who had climbed up on to the roof-terrace and now exclaimed : " *Le voilà ! Le camion arrive !* "

That shapeless mass, reeling and swaying drunkenly down the little lane, was my approaching furniture ? I could not, would not believe it. I had arranged with Emilia and my gardener that Monsieur Périgord should first bring the linen, kitchen utensils, garden tools—everything, in fact, that ran no risk of damage. After that he would return to the Domaine for the furniture, which could then be carefully packed in the empty lorry so that fragile legs of tables, mirrors, and suchlike would not be broken or crushed. I had purposely engaged Monsieur Périgord and his lorry for the whole day so that the removal of my possessions could be effected in safe and leisurely manner, if necessary in four or five loads, since the Domaine lay only a few kilometres from my new home.

Why had my instructions been disobeyed ? For quite obviously Monsieur Périgord had brought everything at once.

As the lorry lurched nearer and nearer I saw with horror that he had indeed done this. The amorphous mass approaching had a superstructure of tables and chairs attached by only one frail straining rope. They hung precariously over the edge, the legs of tables catching in the branches of trees, and my gardener, balancing himself upon the running-board of the lorry and clinging also to that rope, ran constant risk of being, like Absalom, caught up into them by his hair. I saw, with consternation, that his face was flushed and his eyes wild. His dirty shirt was soaked with sweat and, horror of horrors, streaked with blood.

WHAT had happened? I was soon to hear. Apparently Monsieur Périgord had decided that his lorry was large enough to hold everything at the same time if two boards could be found to project beyond the back of the lorry to support any objects which could not be stacked conveniently within it. Naturally, the work of loading had been long and arduous and was but half finished when the hour of noon had struck, paralysing, as it always does, the limbs and members of all Provençaux save for their tongues, teeth, and jaws.

Périgord, my gardener, and another helper had then partaken of lunch, and, as I gathered later, Emilia had served them bountifully with wine to encourage them to fresh effort, a fatal thing to do at mid-day under a hot sun.

When they had feasted sufficiently the work of reloading had begun again, and Emilia, thinking that her responsibility as hostess was now over, had rushed into the house and got busy with duster and broom, trying to rearrange the remaining furniture into some semblance of order and comfort. So that she had not witnessed the departure of the lorry.

Once outside the gates of the Domaine, Périgord, suddenly realising that he was already over three hours late, rashly tried to speed up his pace. The road being rough and untended, my gardener, fearing the worst, warned him to drive more carefully, but Périgord ignored his caution, and as they neared the bend of the road the worst that could happen happened.

A small drainage canal had been cut across the road at this point to enable the rains to flow off it into someone else's property. Périgord drove over this rut at full speed, and the ensuing shattering bump broke the two projecting boards at the back of the lorry, and my furniture, posed thereon, cascaded into the road at the same moment that the lorry skidded into the wall.

Périgord jammed on his brakes just in time to save his radiator, and then my gardener scrambled up the wall, and from that elevation tried to steady and secure the toppling superstructure while Périgord picked up my mangled furniture with his assistant. Whilst striving to stack it on the lorry, my gardener had somehow contrived to impale himself upon a metal spike of a neighbouring gateway. Hence the bloody shirt.

For some time they had all struggled with the swaying mountain of furniture, which mountain had now become a volcano, spitting forth household effects every time they were placed upon its peak ; and in the end it was necessary to unload them into the lane and start stacking them all over again.

No wonder we had waited, and waited, and waited for the arrival of that lorry.

The same catastrophe occurred no less than three times when at length they reached the *Route Nationale* which leads to Nice ; and on the main road the reloading had been even more difficult because of the constant stream of traffic.

I never saw a man more frightened and ashamed than my gardener, who was in tears when he loosed his hold of that supporting rope, tottered into the courtyard, and explained their late arrival. Périgord, laughing and red-faced, tried to brazen matters out. The whole fault lay, not with him, but with the two rotten planks that he had found in my Domaine garden which had let him—and my furniture—down. Not one word of apology or regret did he utter as he loosed that rope and my possessions fell in a final cataract into the courtyard.

I saw tables without legs, chairs without seats ; everything I looked at was damaged or chipped, and a bundle of painted planks, spiky with nails, was all that remained of my kitchen cupboards and dresser.

I was so frightfully angry that I simply dared not speak. Leaving the men to collect the *débris*, I turned silently away and walked blindly down to the Château, there to calm myself by working at my typewriter for two solid hours, forcing my mind to concentrate upon something else until I felt sane and quiet enough to open my mouth and tell Mademoiselle of the catastrophe.

Périgord, having disobeyed my instructions and having ruined my furniture, had only leaned against the wall and laughed in my face when he explained what had happened ; this was what had so upset me. If he had confessed that he had been a fool to think that he could accomplish the removal of my things in only one load, if he had expressed one word of regret for the wreckage of my things caused by his own assurance and stupidity, I should have been disarmed at once. But no—nothing. I poured all this into the sympathetic ear of Mademoiselle when I could sufficiently control the angry trembling of my lips. She listened in silence, but her eyes and gestures expressed much.

" Oh ! your poor, poor furniture ! " she wailed at last. " I could cry." Then, her practical self asserting itself once more, she said : "But of course you've got an All-Risks insurance and that damage is covered."

I had ; but my American man of law explained to me that it only covered damage that might occur in the Domaine itself ; and thinking that no harm could possibly come to my things if they were transported in several loads just for that short distance, I had not bothered to insure them during their transport to the cottage. Therefore they were not ' covered,' and I was properly stung.

My lawyer suggested writing at once to Périgord to inform him of the approximate price that would be asked for the repair of my furniture, and to tell him that his insurance company must pay for the damage his carelessness had caused.

"If he isn't insured, at any rate my letter ought to scare him stiff, and that will do him a power of good. I'll sure put it over him hot and strong," quoth my American friend ; "and don't you dare pay him one cent for hire of his lorry," he commanded me sternly.

Apparently he did put it over Périgord, for one Sunday morning, when I was peacefully feeding Mademoiselle's baby chickens, I suddenly saw Périgord himself, clad in his Sunday-best, standing outside the wire of the hen-run, lying in wait for me.

So startled was I by this black and unexpected apparition that I bolted into the broody hen-house and shut the door, there to remain in hiding until, as I fervently hoped, it would tire of waiting and vanish.

But it did not. It remained relentlessly standing outside the only exit of the hen-run, and if I were not to remain inside until I became broody myself, I must go out soon and face that pig of a Périgord.

A wail of " Madame ! Madame ! " broke the fusty silence of my prison, and, thinking I detected a note of penitence in that voice, I nerved myself for the encounter and went out.

A transformed Périgord greeted me humbly. He had been careless and wrong to think that he could stack all the beautiful possessions of Madame into one load, he now confessed. He saw it now ; saw it only too clearly. He ought never to have attempted to remove furniture, for his lorry was not insured for furniture removals, only for the transport of manure and wood. Henceforth he would never undertake the removal of other people's possessions. He had learned his lesson. How much did he owe Madame for the repair of her damaged things ? He was a poor man, but somehow, he supposed, he must pay for this.

217

Here he suddenly dissolved into tears. Noisy sobs mingled with the conceited cacklings of laying hens who advertised their achievements. Monsieur Périgord buried his face in a red bandana handkerchief and sobbed in the sunshine, while I stood like an awkward schoolgirl, tongue-tied before him, for the sight of a man in tears always has power to unnerve me. I found myself timidly patting the shaking shoulder of Périgord whilst assuring him that accidents happened to us all, and that since he expressed his regret for what had happened, I was ready to forgive, even if my patched-up furniture would never allow me completely to forget that disastrous household removal. But, remembering the admonition of my lawyer, I mustered enough strength to suggest that since I must pay for my own repairs, it would be unreasonable for him to demand his fee for the hire of his lorry.

His face, wet and smiling, instantly appeared from the folds of his Communist handkerchief, and a horny hand was enthusiastically outstretched.

I took it and shook it, and Monsieur Périgord almost skipped down the drive.

When I entered the Château I found Mademoiselle rolling about in helpless paroxysms of laughter upon the divan in the *salon*. " Oh ! " she gasped. " OH, how divine ! I wouldn't have missed that little scene for worlds. I saw it all from the bath-room window. First I heard such curious sounds that I feared one of my cockerels must be suffering. Then I looked out and saw Périgord—*Périgord* in floods of tears—it was his sobs that had attracted my attention. And there you stood, poor darling, regarding him with great compassionate eyes, while he worked upon your feelings to his own advantage ; for of *course* you've forgiven him everything—I saw those little pats, and, at one moment, thought you were going to kiss him. . . ." Here she was interrupted by another irreverent spasm of laughter.

" The poor man really *was* sorry," I pleaded.

" Oh *yes*, sorry for himself ; very, very, very sorry for himself. But now I'm sure you've comforted him and sent him home happy," she mocked me gently.

" I was very firm about not paying for that lorry," I said defensively.

" Well, that's always something," she coun-tered ; " we can deduct 100 francs from your bill of repairs, which will, I fear, amount to some thousands. You know Périgord is *much* richer than you or I."

" Well, anyway, there's always dear Pierre," I said, referring to my giant carpenter. " He was so sweet and sympathetic when he saw that awful mess, and he has already mended all the kitchen cupboards. And there's something about these Provençaux — they are so childlike, and they've so much heart that one can never be angry with them for very long."

Mademoiselle twinkled at me silently for a moment and then said : " All the same they are very exhausting, especially in this great heat, and you look as I feel, rather like a sucked orange. I think the moment has very nearly come when we can put the workmen on to the outside wall and then run away again. It will take them at least six weeks and is perfectly straightforward work, so that our minds would be at ease and our bodies do need bracing."

I agreed eagerly, for I did feel exactly like an orange that has been fiercely sucked by a child.

I felt as if all my vitamins, milk of human kindness—now I'm mixing metaphors, I mean juice— imagination, and patience had been squeezed, sucked, pinched, and torn from me, and I, too, longed for escape.

Well, directly we had solved our lighting and plumbing problems I would find a guardian for the cottage, send Emilia off on her holiday, and then we could go away somewhere for ours.

This *déménagement* from the Domaine had just about finished me.

# CHAPTER XIII.

ITALIAN SPAGHETTI.

FINDING a guardian for my cottage proved to be more difficult than I had imagined. Every woman that I interviewed was scared of living alone and required a male guardian for herself also ; until at last came Irma, a tall Italian peasant of late middle age. I interviewed her—if making faces and waving one's arms can be called interviewing— in a neighbouring town. She came to the *rendez-vous* hatless, as is the custom of Italian peasant women, and with her possessions tied up in a handkerchief. She was getting old, but still looked very active and was quite beautiful. She smiled upon me throughout the interview, displaying a double row of perfect teeth, and, when she considered that I had grimaced and gesticulated enough, she quietly got into my waiting car and sat down, courteously inviting me to follow suit with a wave of her brown arm.

Evidently I had given satisfaction and she had decided to live with me. That was already something, and it seemed that I had no choice in the matter since she had made up her mind and was as entirely ignorant of French or English as I was of Italian.

As we drove homewards, though wondering in great trepidation how I should ever manage to order food or instruct Irma in the ways of my house, I was nevertheless reassured by her expressions of rapture as we left the town and emerged into mountainous country.

" *Bella!* *BELLA!* " she exclaimed at intervals. " *Molto Bella!* " and I realised that our country life would appeal to her.

Arrived at our destination, we entered my little olive grove on foot, whereupon, to my delight, Irma threw her bundle upon the grass and flung her arms around an olive tree, stroking its silvery bark lovingly with both hands and leaning her head against its trunk whilst tears of joy filled her eyes. She had been working in a town, and being country-bred, had nearly died of home-sickness. All this I learned (through others) later.

Then began one of the most agitating periods of my existence, for Irma was painfully anxious to please me, and I had to try to explain to her how to do it. Because I could not understand what she said she imagined that I must be deaf and followed me everywhere roaring and shouting unintelligible Italian into my suffering ears. I bolted myself into my bathroom, the only place left in the world where I was sure of privacy, and with an Italian-English dictionary, a notebook and pencil, I looked up soothing and admonitory words such as *dolce, lentamento, sotto voce,* then emerged and fired them at her.

Her voice did lower somewhat, and she disappeared into her kitchen and I into my studio, where, with a great sigh, I settled down to write. Hardly had I covered a page when there was a thunderous knock at my door, followed by the dreaded voice of Irma calling, " *Permesso ?* " which, I concluded, meant that she desired to enter.

I bade her come in, and she appeared with a gory piece of raw meat, which she brandished before my startled gaze and then let forth another flood of Italian.

Evidently she wanted me to tell her how I would like it cooked. There was nothing for it but to leave my writing, descend into the kitchen and demonstrate, since I could not explain.

This I did, returning wearily to my studio to settle down once more and try to recapture that interrupted train of thought.

I succeeded in writing two more pages before

hearing another knock at my door and a repetition of that "*Permesso?*"

This time Irma brought with her a half-cooked cauliflower, steaming in a saucepan—and if there is a more noisome smell than that of a cauliflower in the cooking I should be interested to smell it. This one perfumed my studio as Irma waved the saucepan about as though it were a censer, shouting unintelligible questions the while to her Signora.

The Signora, with as much patience as she could muster, for it would be cruel to crush that eager woman so anxious to please, once more accompanied her to the kitchen and gave a demonstration as to how cauliflower-*au-gratin* was made.

Five times that morning was this performance repeated. At least I was sure that eventually there would be something to eat, for I was constantly being introduced to my food like Alice in Wonderland, "Mutton—Alice. Alice—Mutton"; but by luncheon-time my nerves were frayed and ragged and I resolved in future, with the aid of my dictionary and an Italian grammar, to write out the menu for each day with instructions as to its cooking. In this way I should avoid these shattering interruptions.

Next day I achieved it. It took me over an

hour to write it out, but at length it was accomplished and I took my clearly written pages down to Irma in the kitchen.

It was then that I discovered that she could neither read nor write. . . .

Irma was a tornado of energy. The house was cleaned daily from top to bottom. The brick floors downstairs glowed rose - pink ; the tiled floors upstairs shone and were so slippery that I tobogganed on mats from room to room. The brasses winked and scintillated. The complete washing and ironing of household linen and my own personal clothes was effected in one day instead of three, with no pause, in spite of my entreaties, to take food. A hunk of bread and a chunk of meat were torn by the teeth of this extraordinary woman while she walked wonderfully, like the women of the East, a washing-basket, loaded with wet linen which was to be suspended from every olive tree, upon her head.

My meals were at every kind of impossible hour, for she had no idea whatever of time, neither had she any memory, and always she served me to the accompaniment of cries of " *Dio mia !* " " *Madre mia !* " " *Santa Maria !* " as she, too late, remembered that she had forgotten to cook potatoes or whatever it was.

One day Mademoiselle, with infinite patience,

gave Irma a lesson in the making of *consommé*. She bought the necessary pounds of beef and veal and bones, and she measured out the exact quantities required of each, even making little heaps of the prepared vegetables to be cooked with the meat to give a flavour, and making little bunches of herbs so that there could be no mistake.

Irma, ever eager to learn, was thrilled, and begged to be allowed to do the actual making of the soup all by herself. Yes, she quite understood all that the Signorina had explained, even to the importance of pouring the finished *consommé* through a piece of fine linen to clarify it and take away all grease.

I wondered much as to the result, which proved to be somewhat thin and washy. This was explained when Irma told Mademoiselle that she had been quite able to make the soup with less than half the quantity of meat, so that now the remnants of the beef and veal would feed us all for the next day. Hopeless.

We could, however, compliment her upon the clarity of her soup, which was beautifully free from grease and solid substance, but our complimentary smiles stiffened and froze on our faces when she produced the filthy kitchen dish-cloth she had used as a filter, this to save unnecessary washing.

I was reminded of a story of my elder brother's.

When he was in Borneo he had a Chinese cook, and one day he found his Chinee pouring aspic jelly through one of his master's silk socks. When my brother expostulated with him, his cook protested that he was not using a *clean* sock.

Well, Irma's dirty dish-cloth was at any rate better than a soiled sock ; nevertheless, we drank no more of that soup.

We tried to tidy and to smarten Irma, but soon became discouraged. The clean white aprons that I provided were used, in moments of emotion, to wipe the nose and the eyes. If it began to rain, they would be twisted into turbans to protect the head, and afterwards replaced, creased into wisps, around the waist.

There was never such a woman for safety-pins. Apparently she had lost every button she ever possessed, and safety-pins, black, white, coloured, or gilt, replaced them. She always kept a reserve of ' spares ' slung together in a chain from her bosom.

I provided her with the usual black slippers for working in the house and with rubber *sabots* to wear when washing clothes or for the garden. But if she began the day in slippers she ended it with them, and a few rainy days ended their short life, for she sloshed about happily in the mud entirely forgetting to remove them and put on the rubber *sabots*. One memorable day she served me and some of my friends at luncheon in her stocking-feet, and I, with eyes on stalks with horror, could count her ten protruding toes and even saw bits of her lean brown soles. Irma was a dear and a wonderful worker, but she was an incurable slut.

Also she was a terrible talker. She began to talk early in the morning and she never ceased from talking during the day, either to me or to herself. Mademoiselle once remarked that it was really a very impressive habit, for guests, hearing this continual flow of conversation in the kitchen regions, would think that I employed a large staff instead of one lone woman.

But much as I liked Irma I soon realised that I could not safely or conveniently leave her as guardian of my house during my absence. To begin with, she could not order food for herself nor answer the telephone when my friends rang up my house ; and her mind was so vague that she was quite likely to leave lights burning all night and doors unlocked, blow herself up on the gas-stove, or go off to a far distant village to visit one of her sons who was employed there and never be able to get back, being unable to ask her way or the hours of the motor-buses.

And so one morning I braced myself to tell Irma that our arrangement could not go on. Laboriously I searched my Italian dictionary for soothing explanatory phrases. I intended to explain her dismissal by telling her that I must find someone who could look after themselves and answer the telephone, but to assure her that I had nothing but appreciation for her good work and character.

I did contrive to convey my meaning at last, and with shattering effect. To my great pain, Irma broke into noisy weeping, and made me understand that she had always thought her present state of felicity was too good to last. One found a Paradiso and one was driven forth by a flaming sword. She had dreamed all night of a serpent, and now this morning the serpent of an unkind Fate had stung her. Unfortunately for me I had begun to understand some Italian.

After this outburst, poor Irma dusted my bedroom with such violence that she swept to the floor and broke one crystal bowl and one antique glass candlestick, and her sobs and lamentations broke forth anew with even greater violence. She told me that as she could never be happy with anyone else in France, she would now return to her family in Italy and send her elder daughters out to work.

When the day of her departure came I had to present her with a suitcase and help her to pack, for her bundle would no longer contain the miscellaneous objects this dear, quaint jackdaw had collected whilst with me. She had a large packet of Christmas cards of mine, commercial calendars presented to me by various tradesmen, and a mass of sparkling trinkets which had decked our Christmas tree. Artificial snow, sold in pillboxes, had now burst bounds and glittered upon Irma's garments. A nearly toothless comb was tucked inside a squashy slipper. The new toothbrush that I had provided was still inside its sealed sterilised case, and, like the six new pairs of stockings I had given to her, had never been used.

A curious fusty smell emanated from a large sack, which she insisted must also be included in that suffering suitcase. I had purposely given her one of the expanding ' Revelation ' type, anticipating the nature of her luggage, but this one had already nearly expanded to its fullest extent, and, if urged much farther, would certainly end by revealing all its contents at some unexpected and probably most inconvenient moment.

I made a despairing gesture as Irma produced this awful sack from under the bed, whereupon she slyly opened it to show me a mass of chicken feathers plucked from the birds we had eaten since her advent. With these, she informed me by expressive gestures, she intended to make for herself a feather-bed.

Chicken feathers should be well baked before being taken into a house—I need not explain

why, for all who have kept poultry will know—
but these had quite evidently never seen the
inside of an oven. I should have to fumigate
Irma's bedroom after her departure.

When at last we had succeeded in shutting
that suitcase, Irma fished inside the neck of her
dress and produced a folded sheet of transparent
paper such as architects use, and, opening it,
displayed before me the ground-plan of a tiny
four-roomed house.

" *Casa mia!* " she said proudly, and then somehow contrived to explain to me that this was
but the plan of a dream-house. So far she had only
saved enough money to build one room, in which
four of her family of nine (the rest were married)
now lived. She had come to France, leaving one
of her daughters to tend three of her younger
children, in order to earn enough money to complete this little dream-house of hers in Italy.
Then they could all live happily together once
more.

In the meantime she slept always with this
architect's plan under her pillow by night and
wore it next her heart by day.

Perhaps this obsession of hers explained her
lapses of memory and her generally vague behaviour. Perhaps, poor dear, she was always
dreaming of the little home of her own that she
one day hoped to have.

# CHAPTER XIV.

## RUSSIAN SALAD.

AFTER this experience I knew that I must find a man to caretake for me, since among all the women that I had interviewed, Irma had proved to be the sole applicant who had not feared to live alone in the cottage during my absence, and she had proved impossible for other reasons.

I began to make the usual wearisome inquiries, without success, for every man who applied for the post was either a chauffeur or a gardener—or both—and I wanted someone who understood housework and could cook for himself.

The heat at mid-day was now intense, and we longed to rush away into the Alps. Every morning Mademoiselle babbled to me of gentians and glaciers, and the very thought of them made us feel hotter still and less able to bear our present condition. I simply must find someone soon to caretake in my cottage so that we could escape.

And then one evening when I was sitting in a sticky state in my studio trying to force myself to write, there came a knock at my private door leading into the garden.

Outside, clad in plus-fours under a light over-coat, stood a tall well-set-up man with a small clipped moustache. At first I thought that he must be one of the English colony out here, and, from his bearing, certainly a soldier. I waited for him to explain his presence at that unusual hour, and he introduced himself as Colonel Strepoff, late of the White Army of Russia, at my service, clicked his heels together, and made a beautiful bow.

Or rather, he wished to be *in* my service. He had heard that I required a *chef-valet de chambre-mâitre d'hotel-chauffeur-jardinier-gardien*. He was, it appeared, all of these things rolled into one.

I held out my hand, which he immediately conveyed to his lips with another obeisance, and I then begged him to sit.

I was totally taken aback and had not an idea how to continue an interview begun so strangely, but he was perfectly at his ease and very soon put me at mine, for he produced his papers per-mitting him to work in France and various excel-lent references, including one from his last place, where he had worked for three years ; his visiting-card and another, striped with the Russian colours, which certified that he had indeed been a Colonel of the White Army.

He had a wife and new-born twins in a town near-by, and he had left his former situation to work nearer to them.

I took him over the cottage, and he was rapturous when he saw the little flat that I had designed for Emilia and which he might perhaps occupy for a time. The idea of having his own personal bath-room overcame him completely. For three years he had been obliged to pay for a hot bath in the town where he had been working, or to climb three floors to have a cold one once a week. He had not been permitted to speak his own language although there had been another Russian in the household; he had eaten scarcely anything but macaroni and beef-dripping, and, hardest of all, he had not been allowed to play his guitar.

If he came into my service, would I permit him to play his guitar ?

I could imagine nothing more romantic than to have a cook who played the guitar and to hear strains of sad Slav music rising from the kitchen on summer evenings. But I wondered if I should ever get anything to eat.

However, as his references seemed to be in perfect order, his manners almost too perfect, and he appeared to be mad keen to enter my service the very next day, I engaged Colonel Strepoff on the spot. When I asked him what I should call him, he told me that his name was Serge.

Serge arrived punctually next morning complete with luggage—and guitar—and I begged him first to unpack his clothes and settle himself comfortably in his own quarters. I had tried to equip them as befitted an officer and a gentleman, with writing materials, ash-trays, and so forth, and was rather dismayed when a few minutes after entering it he reappeared to ask me what aspect his bedroom had and whether the window faced east.

My heart sank within me. I was very vague as to the points of the compass, but it seemed that his room did not please him. He was going to be difficult.

Nervously I fetched a compass and gave it to him. His face lit up with a happy smile. All he wanted was to place his ikon facing east, and he disappeared, beaming, into his room.

Later, he invited me to enter it. In a corner, facing east, he had affixed a silvered bracket, upon which was placed his ikon with a little oil *veilleuse* lamp burning before it. Draped behind was a tattered Russian flag. He tenderly pulled out its folds to show me the places where Communist bullets had pierced it, and then pointed to dents in the silver ikon, also caused by shot.

"That is the flag of my armoured car," he told me proudly. "That, and my ikon, went with me everywhere throughout two wars, and my ikon, carried in my breast pocket, saved my life. Here, and here, the bullets hit it, but they never touched the face of the *Sainte Vierge*."

Below the ikon were pictures of the late Tzar, the Tzarina, and the Tzarevitch. In another corner of the room hung his guitar.

"I made the woodwork myself," he told me, "and my Captain arranged the strings and keys so that I can obtain a sob like that of an Hawaiian guitar. I am so happy here already," he suddenly confided to me. "Here I feel that my soul can expand. Here I can at last be myself." Then, bursting suddenly into English, he said with a smile, "Eet ees so cozee."

I wanted the cottage to be cosy, and his quick appreciation of its atmosphere pleased me.

"I am also a carpenter and an engineer," he now informed me, producing a bag of workman-like tools from his suitcase. "If there are any small repairs to be done in the house I shall always do them. The house of Madame must be quite perfect. To-morrow she will doubtless show me her car. For the last three years I have driven a Rolls, a Peugeot, and a Renault."

I left him to finish his unpacking, and sped

down to the Château to tell Mademoiselle all about my admirable (Colonel) Crichton.

" I'm sorry he's got a soul needing expansion," she commented, to my disappointment. " I only hope he won't spend his time expanding it and playing the guitar instead of cleaning your house. I know these Russians. They can be perfectly charming and very eloquent, but they are the least practical people in the world and terribly temperamental."

She herself had employed one for some time, during which he had tamed a marauding mouse which had cleverly evaded the hunting of sporting Squibs and the mouse-traps of Mademoiselle and had persisted in eating her stores. For weeks she had tried to capture that mouse. Alexandre, her Russian, informed her one day that the mouse was his greatest friend, sat at his feet daily, and shared his meals in the kitchen. All the cats and dogs of the neighbourhood that prowled around the Château were encouraged in like manner.

" *Tout le monde a le droit d'avoir une vie,*" asserted Alexandre in his quaint French.

In the end he departed, saying that his soul was stifled indoors and that he must find work in the open air where it could breathe and expand.

Mademoiselle, who had found him in a destitute condition, had equipped him from the skin outwards at much expense, and had tried to give him a happy home and much liberty, and had reason thereafter to fear the souls of Russians.

"Your man may prove an exception to the Russian rule," she tried to console me. "But—always remember Alexandre. He was typical."

I argued that the Russian cook who was installed in the house of Tucker's mistress seemed to be hard-working enough although full of poetry and sentiment. I reminded her of the great chocolate cake prepared for a young visitor's birthday with her name written upon it, and how, when the day of her departure came and the cake was still unfinished, the remaining portion of it had been re-iced and the farewell message " Bon Voyage " inscribed in glacé cherries. Pretty manners combined with economy. What could be more excellent ? The cake had served two purposes.

"And surely you can't have forgotten that marvellous Russian salad he prepared on Jubilee Day, with God save the King written around it in mayonnaise sauce ? " I pressed Mademoiselle, who laughed at the recollection and teased me no more.

Nevertheless, I did feel rather nervous of this new experiment, never before having had personal dealings with Russians, and, of course, all the stories I had heard of them began to flood into my mind. I remembered one, told me by a French doctor, about a family of Russian refugees who were given shelter by a rich American. There came a day when one of the Russians fell ill and this doctor was called in to examine the sufferer. He counselled an immediate operation, and made all arrangements for it to be performed in his own hospital at ten o'clock next morning.

The benevolent American lent the Russian family his car in order that they might accompany the patient to the hospital and see him comfortably installed.

At ten o'clock next morning the doctor, surgeon, anæsthetist, and nurses were ready equipped and waiting in the operating theatre, but no Russians appeared. An urgent telephone call assured the matron that the family had left in their host's car an hour ago. The drive should only have taken them half an hour. Doubtless the car had broken down in some mountain road.

The hospital staff waited for another half-hour, and then, as the Russian patient never arrived, they proceeded to perform other duties.

At ten o'clock that night the Russian was delivered at the hospital in an exhausted condition. His family had decided to profit by the loan of this luxurious car and to spend an exciting day at the Casino at Monte Carlo. They had left the patient in the car while they gambled, with the few francs left to them, for the whole day.

When admonished for the heartlessness of their behaviour they protested, in hurt surprise, that they had hoped to win a great deal of money with which they could have bought comforts for their invalid—" could have bought "—for, of course, they had lost.

At the same time, I was told another story of a Russian lady who fell ill in one of the Riviera towns. The English colony, knowing that the illness must be a long one and that the family had no resources, clubbed together and raised a sufficient sum of money to provide an English trained nurse for several months.

When three months had expired, the English lady who had collected the money thought that it might be well to visit the Russian family and find out if the services of the trained nurse would still be required for a longer time.

She found the patient in bed—a very untidy bed—and she had great difficulty in reaching it because of the stacks of dirty plates, dishes, cups, and glasses strewn and piled upon the floor. The room showed every sign of complete neglect and of social entertaining, but there was no sign of the English trained nurse : only a ragged old Russian woman dozing in a chair by the window.

When asked for an explanation, the Russian family told their visitor that they had considered it to be a better and more practical plan to divide the money collected for the fees and food of the English nurse between their impoverished friends and relations, who had taken turns to watch by the sufferer's bed. In this way the invalid had never once been lonely, and many Russians had been fed.

I repeated these stories now to Mademoiselle, telling her that I could hardly believe them to be true. She laughed heartily and assured me that they must be, for they were perfectly characteristic of the Russian method of reasoning. I could only hope that my Russian might prove to be a little different.

That evening, after he had cooked and served our dinner nervously but well, I asked my Colonel if he would play to us on his guitar. Mademoiselle had told me that until he had done this he would never feel at home.

" Put him in a chair before a log-fire and leave him alone—then listen," she advised me.

When I made the suggestion his whole face became radiant. First, he must wash up the dishes, and after that nothing would give him more delight than to play his beloved guitar ; and presently he reappeared carrying it with him.

I placed him opposite a fire of olive logs in the hall-room (up in our mountains one is nearly always glad of a fire in the evening), Mademoiselle and I sat in the little adjoining *salon* so that our near presence should not make him feel self-conscious, and soon he began idly to finger the guitar-strings, striking minor chords and fingering light arpeggios until gradually a plaintive Russian melody stole upon our ears.

He played—and played—and after a time, losing himself in his music, he began softly to croon the haunting melodies to himself, and finally began to sing.

Not a powerful nor trained voice, but perfectly true, and we listened entranced, hardly moving and never speaking, so that he totally forgot our presence as he played one Slav song after another, never touching a false note.

" If he works as well as he plays . . .," I whispered to Mademoiselle.

At length, with one last sob of the guitar, he ceased, and then we thanked him for an hour of enchantment.

" I saw visions in the fire," he confessed dreamily. So the psychology of Mademoiselle had been true.

My Colonel proved later that he could work as well as play. His military training had taught him to be more or less methodical, and he could obey an order without argument—a thing rare in Russians, I am told.

He rather wearied me with little Russian maxims and precepts, which he quoted continually—the equivalent of the English "A place for everything and everything in its place," "Never put off till to-morrow what can be done to-day" (although he had a marked tendency to do this), and so on. He told me that his wife described him as a *vielle fille* because he was so fussy over detail.

I also found it sometimes tiresome and always painful when he reminisced about past days in Russia. While cleaning the silver he would sigh over the stolen plate of the Strepoffs ; or he would suddenly enter my room to show me an old tight-waisted photograph of himself in uniform ; and once, when the *coiffeur* came up to shampoo the heads of the English colony, Serge brought me a package, folded in layer upon layer of tissue-paper which, when slowly and reverently removed, displayed a plait of hair cut from the head of his wife after her confinement. He was very near tears.

It was rather exhausting in that heat always to be expected to pour forth sympathy and appreciation. If supplied continually with these he worked happily and well, but one could never evade the personal note, which rather embarrassed me.

It takes time to accustom oneself to have one's hand kissed night and morning by one's cook ; to be informed with a low bow that one is looking *chic* in a certain costume just as one is about to order food ; to be obliged to listen sympathetically to long stories of the old life in Russia in the days when my Colonel cook employed a large staff himself. He was ready and willing to do any and every kind of work, but he could not let me forget for a moment that he had been a landed proprietor and a Colonel of the White Army in Russia.

A pity, for a really good actor must entirely forget himself when playing a part. He must BE the individual whom he impersonates.

However, the work went passably well. Serge had not had much experience with cooking, but adored making adventurous experiments, dragging up herbs and leaves from the mountain-side to put into his soups and sauces and preparing curious salads of fruits and vegetables. It was interesting and amusing to see what new combinations of foods he would try next ; they were often queer but never unpalatable, and I encouraged his initiative. Everything he made he described to me as *"Magnifique!"* which left no room for higher praise from me.

He had a feminine love of flowers, with which he filled my rooms. A vase of flowers was always set before me when I ate, others arranged before the pictures of my mother and "Monsieur," while single blossoms floated in the finger-bowls at dessert. I had not at first the heart to tell him that he had usurped my greatest pleasure and privilege; that I did not admire his mixtures of colour, and that sometimes he picked my choicest flowers which I was jealously hoarding for seed; for it was all done with such intense enjoyment of things beautiful, and he was always so naïvely delighted with his own taste and sensibility.

In spite of this artistic temperament of his, he was fairly thorough in his cleaning of the house, and his kitchen was always spotless and neat. He told me that he had been brought up in one of the German colonies in Russia, and it was there that method and love of cleanliness had been instilled into him.

Also he was a fairly good chauffeur, as I found out presently when he had at last persuaded me to let him drive me in *Desirée*. I had for so many years been my own chauffeuse that when at last I consented to be driven it was with some apprehension.

My chauffeur, when seen at full length, had a somewhat odd appearance. I had bought him a proper chauffeur's hat; he had a clean collar and shirt of his own; a blue woollen pullover served as waistcoat, and a well-worn black jacket covered it. Below that were blue linen trousers. But when seated in the car, with only his head and shoulders visible, he looked quite smart.

I came downstairs that morning prepared for my drive, but quite unprepared for my ceremonious greeting by Colonel Strepoff. There he stood, beside *Desirée*, my car, who shone and sparkled from unwonted attentions, for it was long since she had been washed and polished. Very early in the day I had decided that my car should be my slave and I not hers, and she had only been washed when a wet day prevented my gardener from doing anything else. For months the weather had been fine, and *Desirée*, consequently, less so. Now I hardly recognised her.

My chauffeur advanced towards me, kissed my hand, and then with a courtly gesture armed me into my car. I felt positively regal, and feared that if my peasant neighbours witnessed this little display they would think that Madame had come into a fortune, and that in future local prices would rise for every commodity.

However, only Mademoiselle saw our departure.

I suddenly caught sight of laughing eyes and mocking mouth at a window of the Château as we drove away.

As we spun along the *Route Nationale* my Colonel recounted to me another chapter of his life story. No Russian can talk without picturesque gesticulation, and sometimes the driving-wheel was never held at all as Serge eloquently waved his hands.

His story was so dramatic, so tragic, and so personal that I felt it to be impossible to interrupt it by a gentle suggestion that the main mountain roads of Provence, with their terrifying bends, need the unswerving attention of the driver. So I clenched my teeth and hands and hoped that my self-control would be counted unto me for righteousness and that our drive might not end in disaster.

At intervals Serge turned his head back and looked me full in the eyes, doubtless to see the effect of his story, until *Desirée*, feeling herself to be neglected, pranced to the left or right, and her sudden movement recalled her driver's attention—just in time.

After this had happened once or twice he suddenly realised that if he tilted the looking-glass reflecting the road behind him at a certain angle he could talk to my image mirrored therein, and this, to my infinite relief, he henceforth did. It was a little less dangerous.

He was speaking of his new-born twins, and was wounded to the soul because a Russian friend to whom he had proudly exhibited them and of whom he had asked an opinion had merely said : " Well—one looks green and the other yellow." They were, it seemed, sickly infants, their mother, who had been a dancer, being more familiar with ballets than with babies.

We reached our destination, a coastal town, without mishap, and I let my chauffeur loose among the shops whilst I kept various appointments, telling him to find a Russian newspaper for himself and any particular food of his country that might be obtainable. He found some black bread, some of the cheap red caviar, some sour cream, an enormous cabbage, and beetroot, with which he said he intended to make Bortsch soup. As we drove cheerfully home he told me that he had had time to visit the General of his old regiment, who was now a *chef* and who had given him many valuable culinary hints. If I happened to need the services of a really good dressmaker, the wife of the General was, he informed me, *une merveille*. They have courage, these Russian refugees.

# CHAPTER XV.

HEAT-WAVES everywhere : the English grilling—
86 in the shade in London ; Paris perspiring ;
everyone in Europe melting like butter ; and
here, in the South of France, a fierce relentless
sun burning up vegetation and human beings
alike. The whole population of Provence gasping.

Even the servants and my workmen had become
irritable ; and Italians and Provençaux are accustomed to work in the heat, and, in general, become
more and more cheerful and gay as the summer
advances, dancing energetically at all the local
*fêtes* throughout June, July, and August. But
this was no ordinary heat, and the little self-control
that peasants have, dissolved in it.

The occasional *bêtises* of Dante, whose head
(covered now by a large mushroom straw hat
lined with cabbage leaves which formed a frill
around his beetroot face) had grown several sizes
larger since he had been put in charge of my work,
and who persisted in improvising little surprises

(or shall we call them shocks?) for me, ceased to be amusing—merely maddening—and my temper often threatened to boil over.

In spite of an altitude of 1300 feet, the air that blew through our *persiennes*, closed early to keep out the sun, scorched us, and we lay on cushions thrown upon the tiled floors in slack attitudes of exhaustion, feeling like the wax candles around which drooped from their sconces and hung despairingly at odd angles, their wicks pointing to the ground. It was becoming unbearable.

Although the old Château was built in the solid ancient way with walls a metre thick to keep out heat and cold, with huge open fireplaces large enough for a man to stand inside them and gaze up at the sky through the great chimneys, and long spacious rooms, even here the air was sultry, and Mademoiselle and I decided that we must at once flee up higher in the mountains in search of snow-peaks and glaciers.

We scanned maps and guides, and we questioned our peasant neighbours in the hope that one of them would know of the perfect camping site in just such a place as we sought. Various suggestions were made to us, but there was always some objection to the locality, and we became discouraged. Then at last Mademoiselle proposed a plateau in the *Hautes Alpes* that she knew and loved, and I jumped at the idea. It took two days to reach it, she told me, but, once there, the air was always cool because of the proximity of four glaciers. It was a very lovely place at the top of the world and carpeted with Alpine flowers ; but as the plateau was both remote and solitary, it would be safer to take a chauffeur-mechanic with us in case of difficulties with the cars. She knew of one, Henri, who would come. He could go and get provisions for us, and might be useful for odd jobs about the camp as well.

With our last ounce of energy dripping from us, aided by Serge, we packed our tents, provisions, and equipment. He was very anxious to accompany us, and felt quite certain that we should meet with every kind of mishap and misadventure if he were not there to protect us.

I had to point out that I had engaged him to protect my house during my absence ; that Mademoiselle and I usually started forth on these adventures quite alone, but that this time we should have Henri (of whom Serge did not seem to have a great opinion) and Squibs as watch-dog of tents.

With tears in his eyes he handed each of us a bouquet of flowers, and finally presented me with an ikon, procured especially from his Russian Archbishop, to protect us from all harms, and two small candles to light before it. Then he clicked his heels together, and, bowing low over our hands, kissed them in farewell

We left him standing stiffly at attention in the courtyard of the Château, and started off in the two cars, Mademoiselle and I with Squibs in my Fiat, and Henri following with the baggage in the Peugeot.

The heat was almost overpowering during the day, but as we climbed higher and higher, so did our spirits, because at last we smelt snow in the cooler air.

We reached the foot of our plateau in the late afternoon of the second day, left our cars in the road below, and began our climb.

Tired as I was, I nearly went mad with excitement when I found that I could not walk a step without crushing masses of precious Alpine flowers. The rays of the setting sun shone through their petals, making them luminous, and I realised suddenly that the true time to see flowers at their loveliest is just an hour before sunset, and the only right attitude—for every reason—is upon the knees.

I sank down upon mine and looked into thousands upon thousands of radiant flower-faces. The plateau was blue with gentians and starred with white Paradiso lilies. Wee farinosa primulæ and cushions of pink silene acaulis clustered and clung to the grey boulders edging the three little brawling glacier torrents which surrounded our chosen camping site. Above it were huge snow-peaks, and before us a great glacier with a foreground of cherry-coloured dwarf rhododendrons. It was beautiful beyond belief.

Then began what I believe to be the ideal existence. For a few days, after cooking our meals, we did nothing but stare at this miracle of flowers and that perfect view. The altitude of 2500 metres made one feel tired and slightly light-headed, but, after the first week, life and energy returned to us. When the sun sank behind the mountains, tingeing the snow-peaks with rose colour, we went into our tents and cooked supper over a little charcoal brazier by the light of candles stuck into bottles. Then, with one more look at that wonderful sky, we said good-night to our glacier standing cold and majestic in the after-glow, filled our hot-water bottles, and crept between our blankets to sleep dreamlessly till dawn filtered through the flaps of our tents and we awoke to another wonderful day.

My first occupation was to divert the course of one of the glacier torrents into a channel that passed between steep flowery banks below our tents. Henri and I heaved out boulders and released the torrent near its stony source far above; then dammed it up where the stream forked above a grassy island. We worked hard and happily for hours under a hot sun until our hands were numb and our finger-nails worn square.

Henri, who looked—and was—very stupid, revealed an unexpected sense of the poetic. I watched him scrabbling stones and releasing the water, when suddenly he sat back upon his haunches and with a tragic voice ejaculated, " *Malheur !* "

I asked him what was the matter, and he told me that the removal of a certain stone had stopped the song of a tiny cascade he had been making. Feverishly he started replacing stones, then paused to listen.

" *Elle chante plus !* " he sighed sadly, then tried again with no success. The whole of our work was held up for half an hour while he tried and tried to recapture the sob of the stream.

In the end, despairing of ever finishing our task, I suggested that we should walk down the bank of the torrent until we heard another unseen singer; and farther down, near a tuft of Alpine myosotis, he suddenly heard again this little song—a low sob under the stones which certainly did strike a note of music. Henri's face lit up, he consented to return again to the question of water-supply, and by luncheon - time we had made a lovely cascading stream, conveniently near to the tents.

Heartened by this success, I became more ambitious. Why not make a swimming-pool near the island ? For two days we laboured in its making, and on the third day woke to find it clear and brimming. I simply could not resist it. I had to strip and plunge in for one icy, breathless moment, and came out glowing all over to dry in that wonderful hot sunshine. It was the most exhilarating sensation I ever experienced, and afterwards one's body was cold to the touch, but one's blood tingled warm in every vein, and for the rest of the day one felt braced and cool.

Our camp gradually became one of the local sights. The Savoyards evidently thought us raving mad to camp under canvas in the *Hautes Alpes,* and the fame of the crazy Englishwomen spread far and wide. On Sundays crowds of peasants and the people of the little mountain towns trailed up to our plateau in a long procession from dawn to dusk to prowl around our camp.

One morning Mademoiselle and I were awakened very early by the sound of voices just outside our tent. So near were they that on first waking I thought they were *in* the tent. We peered cautiously through the flap and saw a party of people, consisting of two priests, one layman, and several women, all talking excitedly together.

The young priest posed his family near our tents.

" *Voilà ! Maman, restes près de la cuisine, et Lucie près des légumes et le charbon,*" &c. Then he hitched up his cassock, skipped across the stream, climbed the bank on to the island, produced a Kodak from under his skirts, and took snapshots of them all in every kind of position grouped around our tents. Evidently they wished to produce photographs giving to their friends the impression that they themselves were living the Spartan existence under the snow-peaks that we had chosen.

They kept us imprisoned for nearly three-quarters of an hour, longing for our coffee, but unable to leave our tents. Although hidden, we felt extraordinarily defenceless and almost indecent in our night attire, surrounded by these people with only frail canvas between us and exposure. Their shadows loomed large on the walls of our bedroom tent, and I longed to poke them in the backs with some sharp implement to give them a hint of our presence, though the frantic barking of Squibs must have told them.

It was strange to hear ourselves and our mode of living discussed within three inches of our heads and be unable to protest, but we could not be angry because the intense interest of these simple people was so sincere, their enjoyment of this new experience so keen, and it was very funny.

At last they went off, chattering noisily, the young priest, who we afterwards learned was on holiday in the village, beaming all over his face at the success of this novel form of entertainment that he had provided for his family.

After that, Mademoiselle suggested that we should ring round our plateau with picket-posts and a rope, call it ' The Circus,' and charge a fee of one franc for admittance to see the sights.

A few evenings later the bark of Squibs warned us of the impending arrival of someone else. We were inside our kitchen tent preparing supper. I was making a salad, and Mademoiselle, sitting cross-legged on the ground, was puffing at our charcoal fire with bellows.

I looked out and saw a slim black figure, wearing a white apron, standing on a boulder and peering towards the tents, and I recognised Joséphine, the chamber-maid of a little hotel a mile or so away where we collected our letters. I beckoned her to approach, and she came up the hill with a springing step like a chamois.

She was enchanted with our camp. She had never seen the interior of tents before, and was amazed that anyone could be so snug and comfortable under canvas. She sniffed our vegetable soup, and laughed joyously when Mademoiselle puffed the bellows and then laid our *broches* (skewers), stabbed through morsels of kidney and bacon, over the fire to grill.

We pressed her to sup with us, but she had already eaten, and would only accept a peppermint lozenge. Whilst sucking it noisily and sociably she told us that a circus had stopped at the hotel for a rest that morning, and that the clients had been much scandalised by the brazen behaviour of a lady in scarlet satin tights who had promenaded the courtyard shamelessly in this startling attire, doubtless to display her very beautiful legs, and who had flirted with all the men.

There were also white lions and an elephant— it was the elephant of the brave Monsieur who had tried to make a tour of the *Hautes Alpes* seated on its back. His way was blocked by snow, and so, being discouraged, he presented it to this circus. It was not often that one saw such a sight up here.

We were saddened to have missed all this glory, and felt that our camp circus was now entirely eclipsed.

Joséphine also informed us that she escaped

every evening after her work was done for a
breath of mountain air and to pick some flowers
for her room. Our camp would now make a
pleasant object for a walk. Her husband, the
*valet-de-chambre* of the hotel, also longed to see
it ; so did the little boy in buttons who was a
French scout, and so did the *chef*.

So we were still of interest, and I began to fear
that even on a snow-peak we could not gain the
quiet and solitude we had come so far to seek.

The next evening, at sunset, we heard extraordinary sounds. Mademoiselle knew what they
were, but I was left wondering, until suddenly
the rim of the opposite mountain silvered with
sheep which streamed down its slopes in thousands
to the *bergerie* below. I had never seen so many
sheep in my life. Each had a bell around its
neck, and the ringing of these myriad bells made
a hollow bubbling sound like water flowing into
narrow caves.

Mademoiselle, who has camped several times in
the mountains, immediately became busy.

" The shepherd will be tired and hungry," she
said. " He will have been trudging roads for days
bringing the sheep up to these pastures. We
must give him some of our soup. I'll run down to
the *bergerie* and see if he has everything that he
wants."

" His name is Bérnard, and he's divine," she panted out to me on her return. " He's got those wonderful shepherd's eyes, blue and clear, and seeing things the ordinary person can't see. He'd adore some soup, and he wants some paraffin for his lantern."

Thenceforth Bérnard became our great friend. Every evening he caught his goat, milked it among the flowers, and gave us a can full of warm frothing milk. I feared that it would taste ' goaty,' but it was perfectly delicious, and the shepherd told me that much depended upon the breed and the pasture. This goat he had bought to nourish his baby girl because his wife had been too weak to suckle her. Crouching before our kitchen tent in that beautiful shepherd's attitude, one knee bent horizontally, the other vertically, his crook resting on the ground and passed between the knees and the arms, he told us that he and his wife had lost four little ones. They came to birth, but after three or four days faded away. Those blue eyes clouded with sorrow, and the sad little narrative was broken by abrupt pauses. He and his wife had spent all their savings on doctors and treatments, but none of them could save his babies. They had almost given up hope when *la petite* was born, but he had spent his last *sous* in buying this goat—he fondled its ugly head as he spoke—and her milk had saved this, his last child. His was a wonderful goat.

I asked how old the child was, and he started one of those pathetic calculations. She was born the same day as that ewe over there—he remembered it because he had to go and find her and her lamb in the darkness ; his dog had told him that something was wrong. The child's next birthday coincided with the sudden descent of the price of mutton and wool—a great loss. That made two years—yes, she must be nearly three years old—what was the date to-day ? The 21st of June ? Then it must be—it was—the birthday of *la petite*.

" *Oui, c'est la fête de la petite Louise,*" he affirmed triumphantly. We poured him out some wine, and for ourselves some icy mountain water, and we all pledged *la petite*.

Perhaps she and her *maman* would be coming up to join him for some mountain air at the end of August, he told us, and perhaps ' *ces dames* ' would fetch them in one of their cars from the station sixteen miles away if the train arrived after the last motor *charàbanc* to the little hotel had gone. Of course we promised to do this, for in any case it would mean a long walk to the *bergerie* from the bus-halt.

Then Bérnard made an hospitable offer. " *Votre chose—là bas,*" he began, jerking his thumb in the direction of the far distant hotel. Our ' thing ' —what did he mean ? He meant Henri, with whom he had spoken on the road, and evidently summed him up as a Thing of No Account. Mademoiselle and I controlled our desire to giggle ; for we were finding out what Bérnard had perceived in a moment with those far-seeing blue eyes, that Henri was not of much use. Never once had he offered to fetch us water or tended our fire or brought us a fresh supply of charcoal. Always he had to be asked to do these obvious things, which he then did willingly enough. The only time, so far, that we had left him in charge of the camp while we went for a climb, he just sat on a flowery bank in the sunshine and read a French newspaper, and when we returned we found no soup prepared and the fire out. Henri was no camper.

Bérnard now suggested that our ' *chose* ' should share the *bergerie* with him and sleep there instead of at the hotel. A wonderful plan that would save us much expense and mean that Henri was lodged much nearer to us. We gratefully accepted this kind invitation, wondering how ' *notre chose* ' would like living inside a ruined *bergerie* in company with about 1500 sheep, several goats, and two sheep-dogs, not to mention other possible lively and minute inhabitants.

However, the new arrangement proved an instant success. Henri loved to be great among the small, and evidently considered himself to be much superior to Bérnard, who could neither read nor write. He allowed the shepherd to cook for him and serve him, and I am sure that the idea that Bérnard despised him in a kindly but contemptuous way never entered his head.

" *Votre chose n'est pas mauvais garçon,*" Bérnard confided to us when we expressed a hope that Henri was doing his share of work in the *bergerie*. When we asked if *chose* sometimes offered to do a bit of cooking, the shepherd chuckled softly and told us that he preferred to *faire la cuisine* himself because he valued a good digestion ; and Henri was just an *enfant gâté*, who had always lived with women, a wife, mother, and sisters, who worked for him and spoiled him.

It then occurred to Mademoiselle that Henri might be put to base uses. He would probably excel at washing up dishes, an art we both detested. Henceforth we made him dish-washer of the camp, and it was the only thing he ever did well and thoroughly.

Before this discovery we had become so bored with his helpless inefficiency, and his standing about with blue goggling eyes waiting to be told what to do and how to do it, that we generally gave him permission to go for a climb in the afternoons, and so ridded ourselves of him.

One Sunday he went off with a party of men who worked in a quarry near-by. They drove up to a certain point in their steam-roller, and some days later Henri showed me no less than eighteen snapshots of himself taken on this occasion, standing alone, arms akimbo, before the steam-roller as though he were its owner; seated in the centre of the group of workmen as though he were foreman. In each picture Henri occupied the most important position, and I peered closely at the last group to see if the cheeks of the other men were bulging, for surely their tongues must have been pressed into them. Then I had a good look at Henri's legs to see if one was longer than the other.

He came one morning to inform us that *Monsieur le Curé*, the young priest who had brought his family to see our camp, wished to wait upon us formally. He came later on and told us that he much wished to find a certain plant—the Genipe —which grows only on rocky crags at a great altitude, and when soaked in *Eau-de-vie* makes excellent liqueur. The eyes of Henri, who is greedy, protruded at once farther from his head, and the shepherd, strolling up at that moment, suggested that they should all go for a climb next day in search of this rare plant.

Mademoiselle, who is an intrepid climber, had located it the day before. We had accomplished a difficult climb, and, quite breathless, I sank down upon a rock. She, however, continued to climb, promising me that she would attempt nothing dangerous without my aid. Half an hour later when she did not return I began to get anxious, and became still more so when suddenly loose stones began to roll past me down the steep decline. I peered up at the peak far above me, and, to my horror, saw Mademoiselle clinging like a fly to what was apparently a sheer wall of rock, and Squibs digging for marmots among the rocks above her, dislodging avalanches of stones which at any moment might fall upon her head.

I scrambled up the slope towards these rocks and found her cutting foothold with her alpenstock.

" I've found the Genipe," she shouted down to me in triumph. " Give me only five minutes and I'll get it for you."

I sternly commanded her to come down before I had a heart attack, and at last she obeyed me ; but she was so furious with me for thus foiling her brave attempt that she refused to speak to me for the whole evening, and all night long mourned her lost Genipe piteously in her dreams.

Knowing the extreme difficulty of finding this rare plant, and, having found it, of reaching it, we were amused when the boastful Henri promised us that if we allowed him to make one of the party he would bring us a large bouquet of the Genipe, as though this were the easiest thing in the world.

We readily gave him the afternoon, and at two o'clock next day the little *Curé* appeared complete with cassock. Mademoiselle remarked to him that his attire was not very practical for dangerous climbing ; whereupon, surprisingly, he kicked one leg high in the air to display heavy nailed boots and puttees bound round his legs up to the bare knees. Then with a broad smile he hoisted those same skirts and kilted them up under his girdle.

They started off, Henri, of course, briskly leading the expedition, though quite unused to climbing. We wondered how long he would be able to keep up that silly speed. The shepherd loped quietly behind, saving his breath and his strength for higher altitudes.

They were gone for hours, but we saw, with some amusement, Bérnard sitting peacefully on a rock near his sheep below the highest peak which Henri and the *Curé* were attempting. He was evidently bored with them.

The two returned at sunset, exhausted and sweating, with a handful of wild flowers among which the Genipe did not number. Very wholesome for the bragging Henri.

I shall never forget those Alpine sunsets seen from our plateau. Flaming clouds like flights of flamingoes sailed over the great glacier against a background of gold and turquoise blue. The snow-peaks were dyed a deep rose-colour, deepening as the sun sank behind them to vivid amethyst. Then when the silver sickle of the new moon appeared the sky turned to a clear pale green and the peaks to an icy blue.

At night, only the sound of distant sheep-bells ; the gurgling and cascading of little mountain torrents ; the occasional distant roar of an avalanche ; and sometimes singing from the tents of an *équipe* of Spaniards working on the roads broke that clear, pure silence.

At dawn we awoke to the song of mountain larks and the fragrance of the flowers—scented daphne, Alpine clover, alyssum, and a thousand pungent herbs. We walked out of our tents into that crystal atmosphere to watch the dawn-radiance transform the carpet of gentians into sapphires and glitter upon the snow-peaks.

It was so lovely that once I found myself sitting in my night-dress upon a great boulder encrusted with vivid pink sedum, playing " Praise God from Whom all blessings flow " upon my accordion, and only realised the eccentricity of my behaviour when a speck in the valley below raised its arm in salutation, and I became aware of Bérnard going off in search of his sheep, which, when left alone, always climb up as high as they can at night.

" Why ? " I once asked him.

" *Sont des bêtes comme ça,*" was his reply.

What a pity that these men who see and know so much of Nature are always inarticulate.

We had hoped, unless we got an S.O.S. from Dante, to stay up in the mountains until the heat below had somewhat subsided, but we had forgotten that winter begins somewhere about mid-August in the *Hautes Alpes*. We were first warned of its approach by a thunderstorm of alarming violence. The air became so still and electric that I suddenly felt giddy and faint. Huge indigo clouds gathered above the snow-peaks, gradually hiding them from view, and our tents were plunged in darkness. Then a terrific flash of lightning illumined them, immediately followed by a crash of thunder so deafening that it left one stunned and shaken—and then began the hail.

An ordinary hailstorm is unpleasant when one

is camping, but the Alpine variety is just terrifying. Great balls of ice hammered down upon the tents, threatening to rip and split the frail canvas. I rashly put out my head to look at the sky, but quickly withdrew it, crying out with pain when the huge hailstones hit my forehead and bruised my nose. In half an hour there was a bank of ice two feet high around the tents, and for two days afterwards our vegetables, stored near the glacier torrent, were buried in ice.

These storms came up without any warning, generally accompanied by a tornado of wind. How the little tents withstood them and remained weatherproof seemed to us a miracle (though, knowing the Scots people, I ought to have had more faith in their workmanship—my tents came from Greenock).

One night we fully expected to be blown with them right over the glacier. We sat on our beds under huge peasant umbrellas in case the hailstones split the canvas, with our storm-coats and rubber boots and a lantern within easy reach if flight to the *bergerie* became necessary. Bérnard had assured us that we could disturb him at any hour of the night. "*Mais il faut tapper fort*," he warned us, because he slept very heavily in his curious Provençal wooden bed, shaped rather like a square boat and filled with straw.

To get to the *bergerie* we had to descend about 200 metres of slippery mountain slope, and in such a wind it would be impossible to hold up an umbrella. But, mercifully, the gallant tents withstood even that storm.

The next day, when we were cowering under blankets nursing hot-water bottles, resting our backs which had become bananas from being confined in tents for three days, and trying to keep warm, we heard the familiar cry of Bérnard, " *À la maison !* " which always discreetly announced his coming from afar off. He brought us the shattering news that his wife and baby were arriving at the station sixteen kilometres away at seven o'clock that evening, long after the departure of the last bus.

We remembered our promise to go and fetch them in this event, and controlled our dismay ; for my Fiat saloon car had been lent to a sick woman who had to be taken back to Grasse, driven by Henri. So we had only Mademoiselle's Peugeot *coupé* with a hood no longer waterproof, which she herself must drive in that awful weather.

We were also a little apprehensive about leaving the camp totally unprotected at night. Generally when we went for any expedition, Bérnard arranged to pasture his sheep near the tents, and guarded them in our absence.  He now suggested that he should start walking along the road, and that we should follow later in the car and pick him up a mile or so away, so that the Spanish workmen in the quarry below (whom he mistrusted) should not realise that the camp was deserted.

That evening we started the descent of our mountain huddled under our huge umbrellas, which soon we had to furl or be blown off our feet.  Once we were inside the car the rain began to pour down upon us through the hood.  I sheltered poor little shivering Squibs inside my coat, and strove to keep Mademoiselle's knees covered by a rug as she drove.

Soon we saw Bérnard patiently waiting by a wayside Calvary.  He saluted us cheerily and climbed into the dicky after assuring us that his legs were encased in leather shepherds' drawers, worn under the trousers, and that he would be quite warm and weatherproof under his gigantic hooded waterproof cloak.  His delight in the drive, and the sight of those blue eyes alight with joy and excitement beaming in that wet face as he peered at us from under his hood through the back window, cheered us enormously.

The drive seemed interminable.  The thunder was so loud and continuous that we had to shout into each other's ears to make ourselves heard ;

the road was a shining river lit by flash upon flash of lightning, and the rain descended in sheets. But it was worth it all to see the shepherd's eyes when the weary little figure that was his wife appeared dragging *la petite* through the station.

They had travelled from Marseilles, where the heat was still almost intolerable. This explained the thin cotton dress of Madame Bérnard, who wore no coat and shivered in the Alpine air. The little Louise was a tiny ghost of a baby; the heat and the interminable train journey had upset her. She looked so fragile that Mademoiselle and I were terrified of the long wet drive for her in that exhausted condition. I wondered if we should get her to the *bergerie* alive.

We wrapped the mother and child in woollen coats we had brought with us, and the shepherd took off his great mackintosh cloak and put it over them both, then held a huge umbrella over them which covered them like a tent.

Only as we were driving out of the station did a howl from Madame Bérnard remind him that in his excitement he had left their pathetic little bundles lying on the platform. They were retrieved, and we drove back as fast as we could, comforted by the thought that the *bergerie* was at least weatherproof at one end, and that the baby would be fed with warm goat's milk near a blazing log fire before being put to bed in the straw-lined store-box that her father had prepared for her, and of which he was so proud.

Having unpacked the little family and seen them safely into the *bergerie*, we threw a tarpaulin over the car and left it in the road for the night, then began the ascent to our plateau, wondering if we should find that our unguarded tents had been robbed in our absence.

But we found that they were not unguarded, and as we reached our plateau we were startled to see white shapes standing motionless around our camp.

Sheep! There they stood, battalions of them, in square formation around the tents—a silent guard. They had even posted sentries outside each tent, and were standing in the corridors between, awaiting our return. I shall always be certain that they came down from the high peak, where the shepherd had left them, to protect the camp for us as we were doing a service for him.

Next day the weather was perfect, and the little Louise rolled joyously among the flowers, playing with the young lambs and going for rides on her father's broad shoulders. It was lovely to watch that little flower-face gradually changing in only a few days from a lily of the valley to an Alpine rose in that wonderful air; but, to the grief of the little family, we told them that we could no longer brave those terrible mountain storms, living in tents, and had decided to go home. They pressed us to share the *bergerie* with them, but it seemed to us already over-populated; and also the thought of work waiting to be done at home disturbed my peace. I must see about curtains for my cottage and I must begin to make it more habitable. I must sort and place the hundreds of " Monsieur's " books now reposing in crates—a heavy task. No, I must go back, and Mademoiselle agreed that I ought.

It took us a whole day, aided by Bérnard and impeded by the intense curiosity of his wife and baby and the helplessness of Henri, to strike camp; and at sunset the little family assembled at the foot of the mountain to see us off, bringing humble gifts, as is the generous way of these wonderful people—a bottle of goat's milk, the leg of a young lamb which had died an untimely death through exposure, and a packet of gentian punctata roots to make a medicated tea.

As we drove away into the mysterious afterglow we heard the sound of a myriad bells, tinkling and tolling, as the sheep toiled up to the great glacier, climbing towards the snow.

# CHAPTER XVI.

FORT ESCU.

BROWN and braced we descended from our Alpine peaks, feeling ready and able to cope with any situation however maddening, but for once in our funny Provençal lives we found that during our absence life had gone on smoothly in our homes. Moreover, real progress had been made in mine. The loggia had been finished and looked delicious ; the courtyard had been levelled and covered with the lovely rose-coloured sand from Roquefort, exactly matching the old hexagonal bricks with which I had paved the ex-kitchens and loggia. The lower level near the great basin had already been sown with grass and divided from the upper courtyard by a low wall flanked by gallant little cypress trees that I had grown from seed, and which would one day hedge in a cool green garden. And my massive outer wall of stone towered majestically, surrounding the two courtyards to north and west. Even the great oaken doors, with their huge hinges and ponderous lock, had been inset, and these impressive barriers, and the square jutting wing of the house with its flat roof-terrace, made my new home look rather like a tiny fort.

As this occurred to me, I decided to call it just FORT ESCU. The French would know that the name meant 'strong shield,' spelt in the ancient manner. I should be more likely to get my letters since it was also my name, and the English would realise that it was a little joke.

The first person I met in my finished courtyard was Monsieur C. No one can pronounce his name. It is Italian and liquid-sounding, like the cooing of doves—Coooocoooroooloo, or something like that, but unpronounceable by the English tongue—and so he remains Monsieur C. He does not mind.

Monsieur C. is a *serruriste* by trade, a man of iron. I refer not to his character, but to the material with which he fashions gratings and iron-work gates for the adornment of gardens; and locks and keys for the security of houses. He had just posed that gigantic lock upon my courtyard door and stumped up now to present me with four enormous keys that he had made for it.

Monsieur C. waxed lyrical over that lock. It had taken him two whole days to understand its working, he confided puffingly to me. It was as delicately made within as a clock and each of its keys turned machinery, apart, which formed the figure 3. It had been a labour indeed to make four such keys—each entirely different, mark you!—for that so ancient lock. Where, if it were permitted to ask, had Madame found that so extraordinary lock?

"I believe those wonderful doors were taken years ago from a derelict *château* near Aix-en-Provence," I told him, "and, fortunately, no one had looted the ironwork."

"Ah!" exclaimed Monsieur C., "there lived real craftsmen in those days. I have shown that lock to all my friends, and it is now the talk of the neighbourhood. Not even the cleverest thief could pick that lock when all four keys are turned. Madame will be secure in her house."

I looked ruefully at my huge unfinished wall. At one end of it my garage would form a completing lodge WHEN I could afford to build it, but at present the wall ended abruptly, so that all who cared to trespass within my property had only to walk round it. At the other end, on a lower terrace, the service-door, heavily supplied with bolts and bars, was held up with but two layers of stones, where one day the wall would be continued. Anyone wishing to enter without deranging Emilia by ringing the bell had only to hook a leg around the pillar of stones, cling for a moment to the stem of an ancient vine, then give a short leaping kick, and easy entrance would be gained.

As I gazed, I caught sight of a leg in the act of hooking—a thick, black leg ending in a squashy-

looking *pantoufle*, which somehow seemed familiar.
It was the leg of Madame Pagini, who, with sur-
prising agility for one of her age, leaped and
kicked and arrived with a flump on the path
leading to the kitchen. I noticed with delight
that the grandeur of the capitalist had worn off,
and that she had relapsed into the peasant state
once more : one that I infinitely preferred, and
she had resumed THE HAT—yes ! AND the handkerchief ! I recognised its wide purple border, and,
as she mopped her streaming face with it after
her recent exertions, I wondered if it had been in
constant use since the signing of the Act. It
looked as if it had.

She did not see me at once, but stood looking
around what had once been her property with an
air of stupefied pride. Then I saw her bend double
and slap her wide thighs with both hands, and
she began to roar with laughter.

" *Bon jour, Madame Pagini. Comment ça va ?* "
I called out to her, and, straightening herself,
she swung round in my direction ; then hurriedly
waddled up the steps into the courtyard, and
seizing my hands pumped them up and down,
chuckling throatily the while. She was loud in
her praise of our work of reconstruction. Never
could she have believed that we could turn her
cottage into what she now described as *un château*.
I could see that she was positively bursting to

be taken inside the house, but was too polite to ask me to show it to her. Of course I took her in, and her convulsions of merriment became so acute as we passed from room to room, starting with the hall dining-room, once the Pagini kitchen, where she recognised the old stone sink, the oil-jar let in to the wall where in olden days she had washed the family clothes, and the ancient Provençal fireplace, that I feared apoplexy. It was incomprehensible to her why we had not substituted *chic* modern fittings ; it was the biggest joke she had enjoyed for years.

We then entered the guest-room where once her nephew and his complete family had slept under that dangerous ceiling, and her rapturous laughter broke out afresh.

" Now I will show you *my* kitchen," I said, leading her down my little curly staircase to what had been the habitation of the goat. Its floor of primrose tiles and the lines of pale blue saucepans and kitchen utensils lining its yellow walls ; its porcelain sink ; and, above all, the gaping square in the wall where the service-lift was to be placed, filled her with awe, as did also the house telephone communicating with my bedroom. I explained that as I could afford only to have one servant, the house must be made as labour-saving as possible for Emilia. I did not tell Madame Pagini that I had gone to this extra expense chiefly to ensure peace and privacy in my home. I had installed that telephone from my bedroom to the kitchen in order that I might telephone my orders to the loquacious Emilia, and so avoid the tempestuous invasion of that fat little person into my room demanding maddening questions of domestic economy at dawn.

The service-lift would further safeguard my morning peace, for, when I had telephoned for my *petit déjeuner*, it would sail up to my bedroom and be removed from the lift by myself. Laboursaving and peace-giving—a blessed invention.

Madame Pagini having devoured each detail with avid eyes, we passed on to the chapel, once the piggery, and here her face sobered into reverence as she devoutly crossed herself before the rustic figure of the Madonna.

" *C'est beau ça*," she whispered, " *Madame a bien fait*," and as we came out into the sunshine she picked a trail of morning-glory whose pale blue trumpets covered the chapel wall, and, opening the iron gate of the little cloister, laid the flowers at the feet of *la Sainte Vierge*.

There remained only the top floor, once the hay-loft, which now contained Emilia's little golden bedroom and bathroom, the linen-room, my own silver-and-green bedroom, shining white bathroom, and lastly, my writing-room, with its colour scheme of blue, red, and white.

As I turned on my hidden electric lights the scarlet curtains glowed and the blue Bristol glass became suddenly luminous, Madame Pagini's legs gave way, and she flumped down into one of my white armchairs.

" *Le tricolor! Le tricolor!* " she gulped as she stared around my room and saw the colours of the flag of France, " *Le tricolor!* "

Without realising it, I had gained a patriotic effect which never fails to break down the reserve of my older peasant visitors, often reducing them to tears.

The tour of the house finished, I led Madame Pagini downstairs once more, and plied her with vermouth in her erstwhile kitchen. Seated upon one of my Spanish chairs, she solemnly drank to my health and happiness, and then departed chuckling to herself and muttering, " *Eh ben! Eh ben!* " as I let her out of that tremendous courtyard door.

Serge, my Russian Colonel, had worked splendidly during my absence, cleaning and putting away all the silver, polishing brasses, and arranging the *cave*, which I had left piled up with every kind of bottle and jam-jar, full and empty. Everything now was neat and orderly. He had fixed up shelves, hung curtains and pictures according to the directions that I had left, and had done countless odd jobs.

I now busied myself about his future, for Emilia had returned from her holiday ; the dear Domaine was sold, and when all the formalities were finished and the purchasers could take possession, she would want to come back to me. I had given her the chance of staying with the new owners of the Domaine, knowing how much she had loved it, but she had assured me that " *Le Domaine n'est plus le Domaine sans Madame.*" And then added, with tears in her eyes, " *Après six ans on s'attache.*" So we cried a little and admitted that neither of us could get on so well without the other, and we sealed the compact in the French manner with a kiss on either cheek.

Her only anxiety was for Serge. She could not bear to turn anyone out of a place, especially the father of a family. She was unmarried and could fend for herself, she said.

It was then that I confided to her that Mademoiselle and I, after a long talk, had planned to keep on Serge. He would be Mademoiselle's cook and man-of-all-work ; he would look after our cars for us and act as guardian for my house and for Emilia, sleeping in the little flat I was building at the back of my garage when I went away at any time.

And so everyone was happy and contented, and Emilia trotted off to catch her bus.

The next day I drove over to the Domaine to

collect Emilia and her belongings. She had thoroughly enjoyed her holiday, and confided to me that she had bathed several times in the sea with her nieces. Coyly she showed me a skimpy sky-blue swimming suit with beach sandals to match that they had given her in which to disport herself in the Mediterranean, but she confessed that she had been ashamed to show so much of herself to all the people on the shore, and so had never worn it.

"*Je suis trop boule,*" she explained to me. She rushed round the Domaine snatching up things she was sure she would need at FORT ESCU until my car was laden to its roof with a mass of miscellaneous objects, and I suggested that as it was growing late we could always drive over again to fetch anything that we had forgotten. Then, at last, with one wild glance around her kitchen, she tore off her overall, slipped on an overcoat, scuttled across the hall, and skipped into the car. . . .

From thenceforth the cottage was filled with cheerful bustle as Emilia scrubbed and scoured and polished and swept out every room, first finishing my writing-room so that I could come up from the Château by day and work in my ' studio,' as she called it. Mademoiselle had pressed me to remain with her for a few days longer so as to give Emilia a fair field for her cleaning operations. The house was now complete, save for the service-lift, and I decided that I would not take up my residence in my new home until it was installed and my peace and privacy ensured.

One morning when I was endeavouring to concentrate my mind upon some writing, interrupted every ten minutes by the arrival of my gardener to ask me some question about his work, or the masons who were building a little hut of bricks wherein to house the electric meter, or by Emilia asking me to telephone for more cleaning materials, there came a knock at the private door of my studio which leads down little stone steps into the garden.

It was Monsieur Pagini—I might have expected this visit, knowing the intense curiosity of the Provençaux, whetted in this instance by the rhapsodies of his wife. With as much patience as I could muster, for I have an especial weakness for Monsieur Pagini, I bade him enter, and, of course, we made a tour of the house together. The moment he arrived, in self-defence I offered him an English cigarette ere he had time to light one of those evil cheroots which would have perfumed my house for days, and fortunately he accepted it, though its ashes afterwards caused him much embarrassment, for he refused to put them into the pewter ash-tray that I offered him because it was too beautiful to be soiled. Instead he collected them all in one soil-begrimed hand until we went out into the garden, where they could be broadcast in safety.

Monsieur Pagini was in reminiscent mood as we walked through the rooms. In this one his son was begotten and born ; in that one he had been laid up for months after falling from an olive tree when he had unluckily ruptured himself. The doctor had given him a queer thing to wear always round his waist, but he never wore it when digging or doing any hard work, only for Sundays and visits such as this that he was paying to Madame to-day. I think he wanted to show it to me, but I hastily turned his attention to the dividing wall between the two cottages which had proved such a bone of contention between old Froissart and himself.

I inquired after his old enemy, Froissart.

" *Ah, le pauvre malheureux,*" sighed Monsieur Pagini insincerely, " he sold his bit of bad ground to Madame for double or treble its value and had hoped to live in ease, drinking pernod every night till the end of his life. But directly his relations heard of the fortune he had suddenly acquired they descended upon him like a flight of vultures and tried to take his money from him."

So wild and worried had poor old Froissart become in his effort to drive off his relations that he had completely lost his wits and had been found running around the vineyards of Mademoiselle completely naked, and no one could catch him. At last his niece, who was also his heir, had managed to lure him back to his cottage, and, once inside it, he had been secured and bound, wrapped in an overcoat, and conveyed by her to a destination unknown, where, it was rumoured, he was kept a prisoner in bed, for she had confiscated his clothes and his fortune. No wine, no money, no liberty was allowed him, and, saddest of all, no pernod.

As I bade Monsieur Pagini farewell after a prolonged visit, I meditated upon the vanity of all human ambition. Poor old Froissart had longed always to make money, to be independent. He had at last achieved his heart's desire and had won what seemed to him a little fortune—but he had lost first his money, then his wits, and finally, his liberty.

I remembered his confidences made to me in a mood softened by four glasses of his beloved pernod in the little *café* after we had signed the Act giving me possession of his strip of olive grove. Then he had seemed to me a pathetic figure ; now he was a tragic one. I wondered if once again I could succeed in finding the place where he lay hidden—and perhaps, somehow, smuggle him in a bottle of pernod to suck beneath the sheets (if there were any) of that imprisoning bed.

## CHAPTER XVII.

### PEACE AND PRIVACY IN PROVENCE.

A ROAR as of fifty aeroplanes. Monsieur C. has arrived in his self-made car to place the service-lift.

Monsieur C. is a man of imagination, and occasionally has flights of fancy, as when he made for himself a motor-car.

First he bought the engine of a derelict motor-cycle ; then three wheels of a bicycle. These he joined together with an iron bar under a wooden plank to serve as seat, and encircled the whole with a kind of sabot of zinc painted canary-yellow splashed with green.

Miracle of miracles, his weird and wonderful car WORKED (as do not all the other inventions of Monsieur C.), and he roared up a stiff mountain road on his trial trip.

That was fifteen years ago, and still his gallant little contrivance carries him and his ironwork to the houses of clients.

To-day is a red-letter day on his calendar, for

he has come to install a service-lift, the first of
his life. I had given him the order with some
misgiving, for a service-lift should be silent, swift,
and labour-saving. I had insisted that it be
small, and that with one pull of the ropes the lift
should soar automatically to given heights, and
that, above all, it should be noiseless and safe.

Monsieur C. had guaranteed all these things
without hesitation, and some days ago an enormous crate had arrived in a lorry, and seven
sweating men had deposited it in the courtyard.

My heart had quailed before it, and I had
awaited with anxiety the arrival of Monsieur C.
That crate looked very large and was obviously
extremely heavy. Doubtless, its contents would
also be alarmingly expensive, service-lifts in private
houses being almost unknown in this corner of
Provence, but Monsieur C. had been vague on this
point. Still, if, coupled with the house telephone,
this lift saved Emilia's fat little legs and gave me
the peace and privacy that I craved in my home,
it would be well worth its cost. And here was
Monsieur C. come at last to put it in place.

First, he must again be complimented upon his
car. He must once more explain to me how he
made it, and give a demonstration of its powers.
One kick of a pedal and there was a deafenng
roar, the engine started, and the foundations of

the house quaked. Monsieur C. regarded his creation with the seraphic smile of a mother looking upon her babe, and then he turned his beaming eyes in my direction, and I knew what was expected of me.

When I had expended sufficient adulatory adjectives upon its mechanism and the ingenuity of Monsieur C., I retired to my studio, there to write in seclusion (as I hoped), whilst Monsieur C. posed that service-lift. He must on no account be deranged during his important work.

But everyone else in the house WAS.

Dante and his mason friend and their two assistants were dragged from their building operations outside ; my Russian electrician, trying effects of light for the last time, for I had said that the night following the placing of the service-lift I would sleep in my cottage ; Pierre, the carpenter, fixing up last shelves ; and the painter putting finishing touches where the other workmen had scratched his precious paint, were also pressed into the service of Monsieur C. That day he was a god among men.

There was a rumble, a hideous scraping sound, and several crashes as (I feared) the cumbrous crate was banged against walls and furniture whilst being hauled and heaved into the house. The din of voices yelling at each other in Italian,

French, and Provençal was heard throughout the day, accompanied by the ear-splitting sounds of blows dealt upon iron. Every man in the place was at work on the service-lift.

It was evening when at last Monsieur C., purple and palpitating, knocked at my studio door. The lift was in place. It worked. Would Madame come and see for herself this marvel?

I went—and what did I see?

Monsieur C. stood before a gaping void in the wall of my bedroom hauling upon a rope. He hauled, and hauled, and hauled; ceaselessly and endlessly he seemed to haul; and as he hauled there was a hollow rumbling and a rattling of chains as the service-lift made its painful ascent. NOISELESS? AUTOMATIC?

Feeling a brute to dampen the fiery pride of Monsieur C. in this, his latest achievement, before an audience of awestruck and admiring work-men, I yet found courage timidly to suggest that the lift was neither noiseless nor automatic.

Perhaps not. "But at any rate it is SAFE," asserted Monsieur C. "It will contain 300 kilos without quivering or falling. It will hold the weight of a man."

To prove this Monsieur C. got into it and peeped forth triumphantly, like a rotund gnome from a hollow tree. The brakes are automatic, he assured

me, and that is what Madame will pay for ; it is
the automatic brakes that are so costly.  A man
could squeeze himself between those shelves, as
Monsieur C. had done, and travel up and down in
that lift, not very comfortably it must be admitted, but in perfect safety, for the lift, when
stationary, could not fall into the abyss.

I feebly protested that I had ordered a small
lift to bring up plates and dishes.  The last thing
that I desired was that Emilia should compress
herself between those shelves as the demonstrator
had done and mount from the kitchen into my
room.

" But a man COULD travel in it safely," urged
Monsieur C.

I suggested that for a household of two a smaller
lift would have served my purpose better, and said
that I had hoped to save my *bonne* work by its
installation.  Had it been automatic . . .  Now,
it seemed that poor Emilia must haul and haul
for an eternity ere my breakfast reached the top
floor.

Ah ! but there would not be a heavy man in
the lift at that moment, only a coffee-pot and a
roll of bread—Monsieur C. concluded that Madame
took only the French breakfast after living so
long in Provence ?  That would not be heavy
for Mademoiselle Emilia.

My sigh was heavy as I realised that the lift was shrieking at me : " *J'y suis, j'y reste.*" It was too enormously heavy to remove. The manufacturer would never take it back from an insignificant Provençal *serruriste*. The weight of it, if thrown back upon him, would crush the poor little man.

" Could it be made to work silently ? " I finally inquired. Supposing that I had an eccentric guest in the room below who liked to breakfast at 6 A.M., must I be awakened by that rattling of chains, that slapping of hauling ropes, and that grumbling roar, as her refreshment soared up into her room ?

A man can safely get into it and oil the chains at intervals, I was assured. The brakes being automatic, there could be no danger for him.

Once again Monsieur C. miraculously compressed himself between the shelves and peeped out at me with moist imploring eyes. His silly little mouth drooped more than ever, his chubby face puckered like that of a child about to burst into tears. Hurriedly I begged him to extricate himself and to oil those noisy chains to the best of his ability. I escaped.

The next morning, on awakening, I telephoned to Emilia for my breakfast. An excited yell from the kitchen nearly split my ear-drum, followed by a torrent of speech punctuated by squeals of delight over this new toy. Actually one could hear the voice of Madame ! But it was so curious only to hear the voice of Madame and not to see her face. Had Madame slept well ? Was her hot-water bottle hot enough ? Should Emilia mount to the room of Madame to open the shutters ? No ? Was Madame sure that she could do it for herself ? Should Emilia order one litre of milk, or more ? And what would Madame like for her luncheon ?

I assured Emilia that all I wanted for the moment was my breakfast, which must be put into the service-lift. Everything else could be decided later. I hung up the receiver.

Five minutes later a rattling of chains and a hollow rumbling sound announced the leisurely advent of Monsieur C.'s *chef-d'œuvre*, and, after a long interval of noise, there was silence. The lift had reached my bedroom. Just as I was in the act of opening the door of the lift the house telephone rang again, and I recrossed the room to answer the call.

" *Le petit déjeuner de Madame est arrivé,*" squeaked the voice of Emilia. Should she come upstairs and take it out of the lift ? On no account. The lift had been installed to save Emilia's legs.

" *Comme Madame voudra,*" in a voice of deep disappointment.

During my breakfast I was disturbed no less than five times by that telephone bell. Emilia wished to know whether the gardener was to go down to the village post office to fetch the letters. Later, once again the rattling of chains was heard heralding the approach of the lift, and Emilia telephoned to me to announce that my letters were inside it. Then she rang me up to apprise me of the arrival of Monsieur C., who had come to find out if the lift were working well. Emilia had assured him that it was marvellous. . . . The new kitchen-stove was troublesome to light. Had Madame ordered any pine-cones and firewood ? The gardener had brought Emilia vine clippings, but they are damp and difficult. Emilia had discovered a pigeon's egg on the window-sill of Madame's tiny chapel and the mother-bird sitting upon the altar. Such things could not be allowed to go on. Monsieur C. happened still to be there when Emilia discovered this sacrilege, and he suggested making an iron *grille* over the chapel window so that it could be opened for air, but thereafter no pigeons could enter and pollute. Also it would be wise to place other *grilles* over the kitchen windows, for a stray cat—which, of course, she had not yet had time to feed and tame, *pauvre bête*—had entered during the night and stolen a side of bacon. Emilia had not known there were hungry cats in this neighbourhood, and one must protect oneself against their marauding until one had time to appease their hunger and make them into pets.

My head was whirling. Where was my hoped-for peace ? Where ? Oh, where ?

I dressed myself hurriedly to escape into my studio, where double-lined walls interlined with cork had been built at the suggestion of Mademoiselle, the ever-thoughtful, to protect me from outside sounds.

Before leaving my room I opened the door of the service-lift. As I bent forward and placed my breakfast-tray within it I was startled by a triumphant cry—

" *Voilà, Madame !* "

And there, at the bottom of the abyss, were the excited faces of dear little Emilia and Monsieur C. peering up and waving to me from the kitchen.

Where was my dreamed-of privacy ?

# CHAPTER XVIII.

## OLD FRIENDS—NEW ROOTS.

THERE was neither peace nor privacy for me during my first weeks in my new home, for all my old Domaine neighbours visited me in turn, agog to see the cottage and garden that Madame had arranged.

They had heard every detail of its position and reconstruction from Emilia, who had daily excited their curiosity while she was caretaking in our old home. I could imagine the gossips that had taken place over the hedge of orange trees which separates the Domaine garden from the property of Monsieur and Madame Hippolyte, who had once supplied us with wood and manure and whose daughter I had driven to church on her wedding-day.

They were my first visitors, and caught me in rear while I was peacefully feeding my pigeons (yes, *my* pigeons, for long since the Italian papa, failing to catch them for himself, had persuaded me to buy them).

I heard a cry of "Madame!" and looked round to see Monsieur and Madame Hippolyte scrambling over my unfinished wall. They had come to shake the hand of Madame and to wish her health and happiness in her new home, and also to show their last letter from *la petite*.

I led them into and around the house, and we finally settled down in the little *salon*, where I plied them with liqueurs and biscuits. Then Madame Hippolyte drew forth a much-creased envelope bearing a Moroccan stamp—the precious letter from their daughter who had accompanied her *chef-sergent* husband to Morocco when his regiment was ordered there.

Before their departure she had produced a son and heir, to the immense pride of the grandparents. I had been apprised early of the coming event by Madame Hippolyte, who, seeing me driving past her house with an artist friend (a man), made a sign for me to stop and rushed up to the car, dragging her daughter Marguerite by the hand.

"*Madame!*" she shouted to me, "*nous avons espoir!*" and she tapped her daughter suggestively, to my intense embarrassment and the equally keen amusement of my companion.

He teased me all the way home, telling me that as I had been roped-in as chauffeuse for Mademoiselle Marguerite's wedding, I should assuredly be asked to officiate in like manner at the baptism of her child.

And sure enough Madame Hippolyte did approach me some months later, saying that it would give them so much pleasure if I were present at the christening, for it would be so touching and so appropriate if the car that had conveyed Marguerite to her wedding should now drive her new-born child to the same church.

Unfortunately, a long-promised visit to friends had caused me to be absent on this second great occasion.

And now I was to hear news of Marguerite and her family in Morocco.

Madame Hippolyte fumbled for her steel-rimmed spectacles, perched them on the end of her nose, and opened four quarto pages of thin lined paper closely covered with fine writing in purple ink, and she began to read them aloud.

Monsieur Hippolyte leaned back in his armchair with arms folded and a beatific expression upon his rugged face. I provided a cushion for his gouty feet.

Marguerite, it appeared, was in clover. She lived the life of *une dame* and had a little coloured *fatma* to look after her baby and help her with the work of her bungalow, which, she said, though small, was very *chic* indeed and had four rooms. Every evening friends of her husband came in to see them, so that sometimes the house was packed with soldiers, and, now that she received so much company, Marguerite had been obliged to make herself a new dress of pale blue silk costing five francs a yard—a necessary extravagance.

Here Madame Hippolyte sighed, and, rolling up smiling eyes, exclaimed, "*Eh ben ! Que voulez-vous ?*" while her husband wagged his head proudly from side to side.

The climate of Morocco was perfect ; the baby thrived and was the joy of its father's heart, but he longed to have a girl also—and perhaps the next time they visited Provence they would have a little surprise to show *maman* and *papa.*

"*Eh ben ! Eh ben ! Que voulez-vous ?*"

Their garden was small, but already they had growing in it two——" Here Madame Hippolyte paused and peered, but was immediately prompted by her husband.

"Two cauliflowers," he said solemnly.

"Ah, yes—two cauliflowers ; six——" Again Madame Hippolyte hesitated.

"Six beetroots—and then comes ' one salad,' " he prompted her again. He knew the letter by heart.

When we had finished the letter of Marguerite and

I had congratulated her parents upon her successful and happy marriage, we drifted on to the gossip of the neighbourhood. I asked for news of Hilaire, our old gardener, who lodged in an upper part of the Hippolyte house. He had never been really well since that heart attack last year, they told me, but was still working for an English lady, who employed him every day (lucky woman to be able to do it. I had lost his services because I could only afford them for three days a week). He was longing to come and see Madame, so Madame Hippolyte told me, and I asked her to beg him to come and visit me his first free afternoon, and then I bade my guests farewell.

Just as they were leaving, Madame Hippolyte delicately reminded me that I had been one of their most valued customers for wood and manure in the past ; and Monsieur Hippolyte informed me that since he had bought a motor-lorry (though he still kept his mule for the fertilising of the gardens of clients) he was now able to stock coal and coke, and could deliver to any distance. He slipped a grimy price-sheet into my hand as I shook his in parting.

On the very next day came old Hilaire, looking very smart in a new grey suit and cap. He had had his weekly shave, which always took ten years off his appearance, but even so he looked older and very tired. He was enchanted to find me on my knees in the olive grove, weeding my natural rock-garden, clad in my blue trousered overalls.

A rumbling chuckle warned me of the presence of someone. I turned to meet a wide and toothless grin, and before I could get up my muddy hands were seized and shaken with violence.

"*Madame travaille toujours dans son jardin!*" Hilaire cried joyously, and I showed him what I had been doing and what I had planted.

"Those are cuttings from the Domaine," I told him. "Don't you remember our planting those agathea, Hilaire?"

Of course he remembered, and how *la pauvre Monsieur* had cut them back vigorously when their profusion had threatened to swamp the geraniums and aubretia on the walls.

The rock-garden at the Domaine had always been the special work of Madame, Hilaire reminded me, and then told me of a fabulously rich Jewish lady who had employed him as a boy and who had shared my passion for rock plants. Every evening she had driven in a phaeton up to a woodland estate she owned high up in the mountains and young Hilaire had led the ponies. Always she had taken with her a little shovel and pail, and, when the needs of Nature had impelled the ponies to stop, it was the duty of Hilaire to scrape up the precious deposit to be used in the wood-land garden. Madame wasted nothing, he informed me proudly.

When they reached the grounds he had to hold a large blue umbrella over the lady to protect her from the sun while she planted her flowers.

"Ah, it was heavy that *ombrelle*," sighed Hilaire reminiscently, "larger and heavier than the lady, and she was *énorme*." He made wide and expressive gestures indicating curves.

What a joy old Hilaire always was with his Rabelaisian humour and store of anecdote.

I inquired after his wife, and he told me that lately she had been working for an English gentle-man cleaning a villa that he had just bought. To his horror, Hilaire informed me in a loud sibilant whisper, a 'bag' had been found in one of the servant's rooms.

"That is the English name," said Hilaire, for his wife, wishing to explain to the gentleman, had asked a French friend who spoke English, and he had told her the word.

Much mystified, I asked what the bag had been found to contain, and then it was Hilaire's turn to look puzzled.

"*Un* 'bag,'" he repeated. "Madame must know what is a B–A–G. That is an English word."

Certainly Madame knew it. Bag in English is *sac* in French.

But after much explanation, illustrated by the gestures associated with the alleviation of irritation, I was at length made to understand that the central letter of this word, the meaning of which Hilaire was striving to convey to me, was U—not A.

The Mairie officials had been called in to fumigate the villa—*quelle honte*—because, apparently, its servants' quarters had been found to be infested with ' bags.'

I felt that the long walk home might tire poor old Hilaire, and so I proposed driving him back. He at once demurred that he could not possibly trouble Madame to do that, but was palpably thrilled by the prospect of another ride in *Desirée*, and could not conceal the delight dancing in his eyes. So off we drove together.

When I had left him at his house I went on into the town, wishing to visit some old friends. To my consternation I found that I had chosen the day of the Annual Fair, and the usual parking place for cars was packed with great caravans. A *gendarme* told me that I should find space in the old town below, and indicated a wide hill leading down from the funicular railway.

Thither I went, only to find another line of caravans edging the right side of the road, and one vacant space at the broad bend half-way down the hill. Here I parked my car and walked back into the town, where I spent a happy hour reminiscing with my friends.

When I returned to my car I was surprised to find a slip of paper tucked under the wind-screen. Much intrigued, I pulled it out and read, to my dismay, a printed *contravention* from the police, signed by *Gendarme X.*, who was nowhere to be seen.

Now what crime could I possibly have committed, I asked myself? My car was stationed on the right side of the road (and the right side *is* the right side in France). It was placed at a wide bend large enough for two—and even three—cars to pass. The place I had chosen was neither a station for motor-buses nor taxis, and it was not yet lighting-up time.

Nevertheless, a summons from the police was not lightly to be disregarded, and I am very proud of my spotless driving licence which, through a period of nineteen years, has had no stain upon its character; and so I decided to investigate this mystery forthwith.

I drove to the first cross-roads and there showed this terrible scrap of paper to the genial *gendarme* on point-duty, and pleaded with him to enlighten my ignorance.

When I had explained the position of my car, he told me that I had broken a law which forbade cars to station at a bend, however wide.

It was then that I remembered my membership of the *Amicale de la Police*, a benevolent society which supports the widows and orphans of policemen. When we first came out to live in Provence I had joined this society, for "Monsieur" and I had always supported its equivalent in England ; and when the secretary of this French society had handed me our card of membership, he had astonished me much by assuring me that in future I might break every law of the town and should henceforth be forgiven. When I expressed my surprise, he shot his eyebrows into his hair and said that it was only fair that we should receive privileges in return for our generosity. A quaint idea this, I thought at the time, and typically French.

Now, after five years of blameless living in Provence, I decided to put his words to the test, and I drove straight to the Mairie and asked to be directed to the Headquarters of the Police.

I was told that as it was a case of a *contravention* I must climb up to the office of the chief of the *Gendarmerie*. This I did, reaching his door rather breathless from steep stairs, and with some trepidation knocked upon it and was bade to enter.

Within a large room were many ink-stained

tables before which sat solid and severe gentlemen in plain clothes dealing with masses of papers.
I looked in vain for the familiar face of a friend,
but realised sadly that this was Police Headquarters and that I had to deal with complete
strangers and was welcomed only as a Tiresome
Interruption.

The most impressive of these unknown gentlemen
rose to his feet and asked of me my business.
Fright made me facetious. Holding the incrimi-
nating slip of paper in my hand, I said—

"Monsieur, although I have many dear friends
among the police of this town, never before have I
received a *billet-doux* from any one of them. I found
this note tucked under the wind-screen of my car
this evening." And I handed him my summons.

He looked at it—and back at me. Then, to
my inner delight, I saw his lips twitch and a
light dawn at the back of his eyes.

I shot a quick glance around the room and
saw that all the other Important Personages had
ducked their heads to hide their smiles, but were
feigning to be immersed in the contemplation of
the sins of the whole local world as chronicled
upon the papers before their twinkling eyes.

The impressive person to whom I had addressed
myself then proceeded to explain to me that I
had transgressed a law of the town. Bends in

the road were, he informed me, strictly prohibited as car-parks. I pleaded the congested condition of the authorised car-parks owing to the Fair, and described the beautiful width of the bend that I had selected, not knowing of this law.

He was adamant. Bends, however big, were, it appeared, *contraventions*.

Then I shot my arrow into the air. I said—

" Surely, Monsieur, you would not imprison an old member of the *Amicale* of your Police ? "

He stared at me, asked me my name, and then walked out of the room—I supposed to verify my membership—returning presently, his face wreathed in smiles. Waving my summons dramatically in the air, he said—

" Madame, it is an honour and a pleasure to be able to render service to a *camarade*," and he tore that slip of paper across and across and flung the fragments with a noble gesture into the fire. He then shook hands with me, and all the other impressive gentlemen rose to their feet and bowed very low as I made my joyful exit.

So is the law administered in Provence.

On my way home, as I passed the little byroad leading down to our old Domaine, I saw, leaning against the stone hut upon which hangs the district letter-box, the red bicycle of my old friend the postman.

But where was he?

I could not pass by without shaking him by the hand and asking how he and his family did, and so I stopped the car, jumped out, and looked about for him. Crossing the road, I very unwisely peered down the alley at the side of the hut—and then I wished I had not. . . .

I hastily turned away and walked quickly back to the car, hoping (as the poor postman had doubtless hoped) that I had been unperceived. But before I had time to drive away he rushed forth into the main road, shouting genially and frankly—

"*Madame! Vous m'avez attrappé! Je faisais ma petite commission.*"

Six years ago I might have been embarrassed, but not now. Life lived among these lovable children of Nature in Provence has taught me even to value their frank simplicity; though it will never cease to amuse me. I greeted my post-man as though we met under the most natural conditions in the world. As, indeed, we did.

I was tired when at last I reached the bumpy little road leading to my new home; but I was refreshed to find that during my absence Dante had placed the marble shield upon which was engraved in beautiful lettering (copied from " Monsieur's " especial alphabet) DOMAINE DE FORT ESCU. The painter had faithfully followed my instructions, tinting and oiling the marble until it attained the ancient mellow tones of the outer wall of stone. And when I entered the courtyard through my massive oaken doors, I saw that the stag's head, the earliest trophy of " Monsieur's " childhood—such a bad head with ragged uneven antlers, but the proud possession of a boy of fourteen—had been placed, as I had asked that it should be, above the entrance to the loggia. Always that little stag's head had been hung above some door or other of every home that we had occupied in England, and when we came to Provence of course it accompanied us, and was fixed over the outside entrance to Monsieur's *Galerie*. From thence I had rescued it, and was now happy to see it once more placed in safety, telling its own short and pathetic story of a red deer of Exmoor :—

> " FOUND OPPOSITE HORNER FARM.
> KILLED POOLE BRIDGE."

I loved it because a nervous, short-sighted boy had thus proved that he, too, was as keen a sportsman as his more robust brothers. I should always treasure it.

It was growing dusk, and already the nine lights of the little hill town perched on a peak above me shone softly like stars in the mists of evening. The one light of our own village, on the peak below it, suddenly opened its sparkling eye as I looked. The scent of jessamine, tuber-roses, and tobacco plant was wafted up to me like a welcoming caress from my garden, and, with a clang of shooting bolts, the great entrance door to my new home was cautiously opened to disclose the buzzle head of my Emilia, who, hearing footsteps in the courtyard, peeped forth timidly to see who was there.

On finding only her Madame, she gave a squeak of relief, seized my hand, and drew me indoors into the hall, where a cheerful fire of olive logs crackled and blazed upon the great grey stones of the hearth, lighting up the rugged boulders that project from the back of it. A singing kettle swung above the fire from an old iron hook ; red roses floated in a shallow crystal bowl on the Spanish refectory table and trailed from my green glass Venetian jar, lit invisibly from below and now placed in the old stone sink. The huge black beams of the ceiling were illumined by a hidden radiance, and Emilia had lit the ancient lanterns hung above the staircases and the ' silent and automatic.' service-lift.

It looked very lovely, very cosy. Surely in such a place one could grow new roots ? After such recent transplantation one would naturally wilt a little at first. . . .

"And the remnant . . . shall yet again take root downward, and bear fruit upward." That was a prophecy—and a promise. . . .

Emilia's bright eyes were closely scanning my face. Suddenly and briskly she suggested what seems to her to be the sovereign remedy for all ills, physical, mental, and spiritual, of the English—TEA.

The kettle was boiling, as Madame could see and hear. In three minutes Emilia would rush up a tray in the *merveilleuse machine* (she referred to the service-lift). If Madame would just sit down and rest in an armchair in the *petit salon*, Emilia would fetch her slippers ; and surely Madame would like a little music on the wireless to change her thoughts ?

So Emilia had divined that the thoughts needed changing.

" *C'est la vie, chère Madame*," she said, standing before me, the little fat hands clasped on the tumpkin. " *Courage—mais Madame a beaucoup de courage. Maintenant — LE* THÉ " — and she spuffled down the curly stone stairway to the kitchen, leaving me alone awhile.

.     .     .     .     .     .     .

There came the sound of scampering feet, the muffled snortling as of a tiny motor-bicycle, and little Squibs hurled herself through the garden door and with a wild rush and leap fell upon me.

311

She kissed my cheek and my ear, she laughed in my face, and her apology of a sheep-dog tail waggled and flickered joyously as though to say—

" Here we are !  We've come ! "

I knew that Mademoiselle, her one precious sheep, could not be far away, and sure enough her head soon poked round the door.

" May we come to supper ? " she asked in her slow soft voice.  " I've brought a lettuce from my frame, and Squibs's food in this little tin can.  She insisted upon coming to look for you.  She has adopted you as one of her sheep, you know, and was frantic when she couldn't round you up in the Château."

Squibs was by this time enjoying an *extase* on the scratch-mat by the door, making the queer sounds of satisfaction peculiar to herself when she is happy as she rolled and stretched and kicked her slender legs.

Mademoiselle sank into an armchair by the fire and looked appreciatively around her.

" How cosy this is," she said.  " Aren't you glad to be installed at last in this divine little safe place ?  Now no one need be lonely any more."

---

*Printed in Great Britain by*
WILLIAM BLACKWOOD & SONS LTD